Contents

Part Two: Finances After Retirement

Introduction

Most people start to seriously think about their retirement when they reach their late 50's/early 60's. They think about how they can afford their retirement and how they can best spend their time. On average, a third of a person's lifetime is spent in retirement and it is a great opportunity to take up the many things that you have not had the time for.

Of course, it is the case that many people have a very clear idea about what they want to do and how much it is all going to cost. There is suddenly time to do everything that you have wanted, within reason and within financial limits.

There are, however, hidden problems that can surface when a person/person's retire. One of these is personal relationships. Retirement can cause stress in peoples relationships as you now spend a lot more time together or one partner retires and wants to embark on different projects whilst the other is still working.

People who live alone may worry about losing the day-to-day companionship that goes with the workplace. People also worry about how they may cope as they get older and ill health begins to surface.

This book attempts to cover all areas relating to retirement. The first chapters deal with more personal matters, including management of the home and future care options whilst the latter chapters deal with more financial issues, such as pensions and benefits. All in all, the reader will benefit from this highly readable book which is packed with information.

Patrick Grant

1

When you retire

Although people generally look forward to retirement, it is true to say that, in the absence of any grand plans, the experience of being at home can take some adjusting to.

Being on your own

There are increasing numbers of people who find themselves alone when they retire. Many people like being single and have planned their lives around this. Although it is true that having a partner can mean that you have someone to be with and to go on holiday with and do many other things with, some people like to do these things either on their own or perhaps with another member of the family.

However, many people on their own also hope that they can find a partner in retirement, someone to share life with. This can be more difficult for women than men. Older women outnumber men, and men may be on the lookout for a younger partner.

The truth is that, in older age, many people will find it difficult to find a partner. The opportunities get less and less. One option is to contact a marriage bureau or to enrol on a dating site online or to go to a dating agency. If you are thinking about contacting a dating agency, particularly for the first time, make sure that you know exactly what you are looking for-a long term relationship or something less committed.

If you live alone, and don't intend to look for a partner, then you might want to develop your ties in the community. A sense of belonging, of community, is very important so as not to get too isolated and so as to ensure that someone will always look out for you.

Your partner

If you are retiring and have a partner, you will need to involve them in your retirement plans. This may sound obvious but by no means all people communicate with each other clearly when it comes to life after retirement and problems can occur. You will have to decide how to cope being with each other all the time, after spending so much time apart when working. If you think that you may need help with the transition to retirement then you should contact Relate who specialise in this area. Many people see relate as dealing only with marital breakdown but they specialise in marital problems generally, or potential problems. See useful addresses at the back of this book.

Sexual relations

It doesn't follow that, as people get older so their sex life diminishes or the desire goes away. It is a fact that many people enjoy active sexual relations for many years after they retire. This aspect of life is just as important to older people as for younger couples.

Most people are able to enjoy sexual relations throughout their lives. However, when people get older sexual expression can take many forms. The importance of an orgasm, for example, may diminish. The main thing is that two people enjoy sex in their own way. As long as fulfilment is gained then this is all that matters. Growing older can bring some advantages in relation to sex. Once a woman is past the menopause then the fear of getting pregnant disappears. For many women, the fact that their partner takes longer to reach orgasm is a definite bonus. Also, when people enter the phase of retirement there is generally more time to enjoy and explore sexual relations.

It is also true to say that sexual relationships don't just involve women. Partners of the same sex equally enjoy sexual relationships as they get older.

Enhancing your sex life

Although, as discussed, people of all ages enjoy active sex lives, it is true to say that for some older people sex becomes less and less frequent. Some people eventually give up altogether, for a variety of reasons, the main one being the loss of interest in one's partner. This should also be handled in the right way. Life together doesn't have to be dominated by sex. If both parties feel comfortable without sex then so be it. The important thing is to maintain good relationships.

There are, however, a few tips which may help stimulate your sex life. A complete change of scene can be exciting. Making love in a hotel room, making love at different times of the day, watching a film can all be aides to a better sex life. You might also want to consider sexual therapy, such as Sensate Focusing, which was pioneered in America by Masters and Johnson. The treatment consists of three phases. During the first phase the couple will be tactile, told to stroke each others bodies, apart from the genitals, telling each other what they like or dislike. At this stage, the therapist will recommend that there is no sexual intercourse. The second stage allows genital stimulation and the third stage full intercourse. If you feel that you would like to explore sexual therapy more, either through the NHS or privately you should contact the British Association for Sexual and Relationship Therapy, address at the end of the book. Age concern also has a publication called Intimate Relations: Living and Loving in Later Life. See addresses at the end of the book.

2

Opportunities available

When you retire you will find that you have a lot more time on your hands, and it is yours to do as you choose. There are many opportunities. People retiring today live longer and will spend, or could spend, almost as much time retired as working. The fact that you will have so much time in retirement means that it is very important that you make the best use of it.

Learning opportunities

When you are retired you can set your goals however you want and one very useful way to use your time is to embark on a course of learning. You can study for your own personal satisfaction, studying, for example, politics and current affairs, philosophy or information technology. You may want to study informally or to obtain specific qualifications, such as GCSE. Another aspect of attending classes, either in the day or in the evening is that you will meet like-minded people. Because of age discrimination legislation introduced in October 2006, (replaced by the 2010 Equalities Act) colleges and universities cannot refuse people entry to courses on the grounds of age, so the opportunities are limitless.

Informal ways of learning
Libraries

Libraries are a good place to find out what courses are happening in your area. Many libraries have also set up open learning centres where access to computers and the Internet is free, or at a very low cost.

Museums and galleries

As well as visiting museums and galleries you will also find that you can attend courses, lectures and various events organised by their education department for interested adults.

Radio and Television

Many radio and TV programmes are educational and certain programmes are dedicated to education, such as the Discovery channel. The Open University also has some very interesting programmes, based around their curriculum.

The Internet

This is, without doubt, a very convenient way to learn with almost every subject under the sun being available. If you are experienced and have used the Internet, and almost every one has nowadays, then you will have access to a rich variety of subjects.

If you are new to computers and would like to enrol on a course to learn more, you should try to find the one that best suits your needs. You might want to contact Digital Unite (formerly Hairnet) which is an organisation that offers computer training to the over 50's. It has a national network of older trainers. www.digitalunite.com 0800 822 8951.

In addition, many Age Concern groups and organisations offer Internet and computer taster sessions in various community locations. You can contact Age Concern's information line 0800 009966 or see the website www.ageconcern.org.uk/ITfor all.

Attending classes locally

One of the most beneficial ways of learning is to attend a class near your home. There are a variety of classes, run by Local authority adult education services, Worker Educational Associations and others. The University of the Third Age is a useful organisation where activities are all arranged by members themselves, often being carried out in people's homes. The term 'university' is misleading, as no qualifications and exams are involved. There are more than 500 groups in the UK (see useful addresses at the back of the book). Learn Direct can also provide useful information about all areas of education and learning. You should phone 0208 466 6139 for more information or go onto their website www.learndirect-advice.co.uk.

Learning away from home

If you are not interested in committing yourself to a longer course then there is also the option of short residential courses, providing you can afford the fees. There are a variety of courses, from summer schools in colleges or universities and also field study centres. You can find information in local papers, travel agencies or in the Time to Learn Directory for which you have to pay. This is published twice a year by City and Guilds (see useful addresses at rear of book) or available online.

The National Institute of Adult Continuing Education (NIACE) also offers useful information (see useful addresses).

Distance learning

'Distance learning' refers to learning by post, radio, email, television or the Internet. Although not everyone's cup of tea, it can be a useful form of learning. The main advantage is the flexibility as regards the contents and duration of the course. The Open University is perhaps the most famous of the distance learning organisations, where you can study for a degree (or not). The University offers a vast range of courses. See useful addresses for more information. The Open College of Arts provides home study courses in a wide range of arts subjects, including music, photography and creative writing. The National Extension College (NEC) offers a wide variety of courses-from maths to bird watching including courses specifically geared to the needs of people who left school without qualifications and have not studied for some time, if at all.

The Association of British Correspondence Colleges can provide lists of colleges and courses. For all of the above see useful addresses at the end of the book. For general information on distance learning courses, or to check the credentials of a course provider, contact the Open and Distance Learning Quality Council (ODLQC). See useful addresses.

Taking a degree

Many universities and colleges will accept mature students on the basis of their experience rather than any formal paper qualifications. Many universities and colleges have foundation courses which can be taken prior to enrolling for a degree course. You will need to pay fees for taking a degree although if you are on a low income then you may qualify for assistance. Students of any age may apply for a student loan to help with tuition fees. However, you can only get a loan to help with living costs if you are under 60 years of age (England and Wales).

The government website www.direct.gov.uk has helpful information about financing adult learning. General information about funding and concessions is available from Learndirect on 0800 101901.

For most people enrolling at the Open University, there is no need for any prior qualifications. However, OU students do not qualify for grants. An OU degree will usually take a little longer than a full time university based degree because of the nature of the learning process. It can take between 4-6 years to complete although this is dependent on the individual student.

For more information go to the OU website www.open.ac.uk or phone 0845 300 60 90.

Getting involved in the community

Whilst people are at work, time for getting involved in community activities is limited. However, when you reach retirement age, there is adequate opportunity to get involved. Becoming involved in the local community can be very rewarding indeed and can be life changing in terms of who you meet and the activities that you get involved in.

Joining a local club or society

The best source of information concerning the type of club and the whereabouts is the local library. Before committing yourself to join any club you should take a look at the programme and attend an initial meeting as a guest. This will help you get an idea of the club/societies activities and to make a decision whether you want to give more of your time. Once involved you will meet many people with similar interests as you and this can be very rewarding.

Clubs for older people

Many of the larger employers will run clubs for ex-employees. These might be the civil service or NHS for example. Local Age Concerns will provide information about different clubs and societies. In addition, active older people are always required as volunteers.

Women's clubs

The traditional idea of the women's institute, that of elderly and stuffy people is no longer anywhere near the truth. Today's WI's are very stimulating and can offer a range of activities for members. If you want more information contact the National Federation of Women's Institutes at the address at the rear of this book.

Working as a volunteer

If you have the energy and the time then working as a volunteer can be very rewarding indeed. It can enable you to put to good use the skills that you have acquired at work, and to keep your hand in. Alternatively, it can give you the opportunity to do something totally different. The opportunities for doing voluntary work are endless. The following gives you some idea of the range of volunteering jobs. You could:

- Act as a guide or steward in a museum or stately home-the National Trust is always in need of volunteers
- Train to be a counsellor for organisations such as Relate, the Salvation Army or Victim Support
- Work with children and young people in a variety of settings
- Work with older people
- Help run a charity shop
- Become an advocate for a Citizens Advice Bureau.
- Become a magistrate or local councillor
- Sit on tribunals
- Participate in governing bodies such as a school governing body

You need to think about what you have to offer and what you really want to do and how much time you want to devote to voluntary work. As stated, it can be a very rewarding experience. You can find voluntary work through a variety of different mediums, such as Age Concern, libraries, The National Association For Voluntary and Community action (NAVCA), volunteer centres, REACH (which recruits volunteers with managerial and technical backgrounds) (see useful addresses) and the Retired and Senior Volunteer Programme which recruits volunteers over the age of 50. For more information about VSO (Volunteering Overseas) see useful addresses. WORKING FOR A CHARITY offers training courses for people who want to volunteer in the charitable sector. See useful addresses.

3

Taking Holidays

For most people who are working, holidays are confined to a few weeks a year. For those with children, holidays are usually limited to school holidays. However, once you are retired, money permitting, the choices are that much greater. There is more freedom and flexibility to plan holidays around off-peak times and also to stay away longer.

In addition, your priorities may change. Whereas when holidays were limited to a few weeks a year, sun, sand and sea may have been the destination. The possibilities are greater when you are retired.

The various holidays available
Activity holidays

In retirement you may be looking for something more stimulating than lying around on a beach (not that all people do that). Activity holidays have a special appeal and there are a number of possibilities.

Special-interest holidays

These are run by many operators. Details can be found in various media, such as special interest magazines or from Tourist Boards, Tourist Information Centres or from travel agents. These holidays cover a whole range of activities, including, for example, sports holidays, arts and crafts, outdoor pursuits, from canoeing to potholing, history tours, cooking, music and languages. These are just a few. There will almost certainly be something for everyone. Another option may be working holidays and the British Trust for

Conservation Volunteers (see useful addresses) is one example of an organisation that runs working holidays.

Town twinning exchanges with European counterpart towns are organised by local groups. If the town that you live in has a European Twin (or any other twin for that matter) you should approach your local council for more details.

Cycling holidays are one of the best ways to explore the countryside. Careful planning is needed here because obviously a lot will depend on your own personal capacity. Look at maps to ensure that you choose a route that isn't littered with steep hills. The Cyclists Touring Club (see useful addresses) can provide information on cycling tours and routes in this country and abroad.

Walking holidays are another good way to see the countryside. The Ramblers Association (See useful addresses) offer walking holidays. All holidays are carefully graded, ranging from the easy to the hard. The Ramblers can also assist if you would like a walking companion. Walking Women (see useful addresses) arranges women's walking holidays in the UK and abroad. Many women decide to go on their own.

Reunion holidays are well worth considering if you have relatives abroad. It might be worth joining a 'friendship club' –membership of Lion World Travel/Friendship Associations, for example, entitles you to newsletters and discount flights for reunions in Australia, South Africa and New Zealand (see useful addresses).

Specialist tour operators

There are a growing number of tour operators offering specialist holidays for older people. Also, the Internet has a significant number of companies which offer specialist holidays. The Internet can also be cheaper. Also, local Age Concern organisations and other groups run their own holidays, usually for more active older people.

Holidays for the single person

As we all know, on many fronts holidays can pose a number of problems for the single traveller. The main one, of course, is the absence of a companion. However, many holiday prices are built around two people travelling. The single person supplement can add a significant amount to a holiday.

One way around this is to go on an activity holiday, as detailed above. However, this isn't the ideal solution if you enjoy travelling around at your own pace on an itinerary designed by you. One company, Solitair Holidays (see useful addresses) offers singles holidays for weekends and longer breaks. There are also other companies that offer singles holidays and these can be best sourced on the internet.

Long-stay holidays

Long stay holidays are best taken when everyone else is working. They are cheaper and less overrun in these periods. April, May, September and October are the best months. Some special long-stay holidays are available during the winter months often at very cheap rates.

A long stay package may be the best option if it is the first time that you are embarking on such a holiday. It can also be a good bet if you are considering relocating abroad and want a taste of the country that you intend moving to. Some package holidays offer a substantial package of daytime activities and other excursions and also evening entertainment. You could take a car and rent a cottage or farmhouse in a village or right out in the country. Many holiday companies offer such packages to suit your needs.

Arranging your own holiday

If you are independent and prefer to stay that way then arranging your own holiday is obviously the best way to ensure that you can suit yourself.

Finding your own accommodation can be done as you go but it is better if you can plan in advance and book in advance. Again, arranging your own holiday can give you an insight into a place that you are thinking of moving to.

Home swapping

If you like the idea of a long stay holiday but can't really afford it, then home swapping may be a solution. You live in someone else's home for an agreed period of time, while they live in yours. When you arrange a swap, it is necessary to make certain arrangements, such as:

- Sort out who pays gas, electricity and phone bills, and also practicalities such as food in the freezer.
- Check the position with your insurance company regarding house contents whilst the visitors are living in the house.
- Leave instructions for domestic appliances and also other information about local buses, shops and facilities.
- Leave instructions concerning contacting contractors such as electricians, plumbers etc.
- Arrange for a neighbour to drop in and make sure all is well.

Voluntary work abroad

Another cheap way to have a long-stay holiday is to work abroad as a volunteer. Voluntary Services Overseas (VSO) takes volunteers up to the age of 75 years old. The usual spell abroad is two years. See useful addresses for more information.

Camping and caravanning

Camping and caravanning is very popular and offers greater flexibility when travelling around. This is just the sort of freedom that many people want. It also can work out cheaper in the long run once you have invested in all the equipment. If you have never been camping or caravanning, it is better to try a short package holiday first. Many people, in a fit of enthusiasm, have invested in expensive equipment only to never use it again. The same goes with camper vans. Always hire to begin with to see whether it is for you or not. If you enjoy the experience of camping or caravanning then you can always join the Camping and Caravan Club (see useful addresses).

Medical care abroad

It is important, if you intend to travel abroad, that you are well aware of the healthcare situation in respective countries. You will need to check with your own doctor about the vaccinations that may be needed in different countries. You are covered by the NHS for medical treatment only while you are in the UK. If you fall ill whilst you are on holiday abroad, you may have to pay all or part of the cost of treatment. Obviously, medical insurance is a must.

There are special arrangements with many European countries by which you may be entitled to free or reduced cost state treatment. To ensure that you receive this, you must get a European Health Insurance Card (EHIC) before you go away. The application form is available from main post offices or you can apply direct (see useful addresses).

Insurance

Holiday insurance should be taken out at the time that the holiday is booked because most companies give some cover in the event of cancellation. It may be harder to get insurance as you get older, as some companies impose terms or restrict insurance for those over 70. You need to shop around a range of insurers to get the best deal. You should make sure that you get all the cover that you need. Information about travel and holiday insurance is available on the Association of British Insurers (ABI) website www.abi.org.uk. Advice on taking a vehicle abroad is available from the AA or RAC.

Home security while you are away

In the ideal world you will not want to give the impression that your house is unoccupied. This is an invitation to burglars. There are certain clues that can indicate an absent owner such as:

- Uncut grass
- Junk mail and free newspapers stuck in a letterbox

There is no real substitute for getting someone to keep an eye on your house for you. You can also use a 'home-sitting' service to look after your home whilst you are away. Always tell the insurance company that covers your property if you are going to be away for more than a few weeks. It may insist on extra security precautions if cover is to be maintained.

Can you afford a holiday?

There may be the possibility that you cannot afford a holiday. However, there may be some help available. Your local Age Concern, local authority or Citizens Advice Bureau might know about charities in your area that can help.

Holidays for people with disabilities

There are a number of organisations that offer help to disabled people who are planning a holiday:

- Tourism for All is a charity that gives free information and advice on holidays for people with disabilities (see useful addresses)
- Local Age Concerns sometimes organise holidays specifically for people who are frail or with disabilities.
- Local authority social services departments sometimes have their own accommodation for older and disabled people.

- RADAR (Royal Association for Disability and Rehabilitation) publishes a holiday guide Holidays in Britain and Ireland (see useful addresses)
- Charities such as Arthritis Care and the Multiple Sclerosis Society, for example, often provide information on holidays, and some have their own holiday homes or organise holidays for special groups.

Holidays for carers

If you are a carer and want a holiday break, it may be possible for a bed to be found in a hospital or local authority care home for the person that you care for. Ask your GP or local social services department. If you need a break yourself you can ask for a carers assessment. Vouchers may be available from the local authority to assist with the cost of care while you have your break. For more information contact Carers UK (see useful addresses).

4

Managing Your Home

For many people, when reaching retirement age, an examination of the home that you live in is necessary. You may decide that the home that you live in will not be suitable in the future and you may want to change, probably to something smaller or in an area where you would rather be. It could even be abroad. There is also the option of moving to a care home, or housing for older people. All these options will be explored here. In addition, housing options for those with limited capital will be explored.

In many cases, those who retire and are considering selling their home will have lived in the property for many years, often raising children there. Over the years, many contacts and friendships will have formed in the community. Therefore, a number of questions need to be asked when considering selling up and moving, or giving up a rented home and moving:

- Do you still have an affinity to the area and is it likely to change in the future?
- Are you still near relatives and friends or have these patterns of friendship changed over the years and have your relatives moved on?
- Is your home expensive to run and maintain? How will this affect your finances in the future now that you are retired?

By releasing capital through the sale of your home and downsizing/moving area will this help your finances in the future? The sale of a larger home and the purchase of a smaller property or renting of a more age specific property can release capital which can be utilised as part of your pension plan or for liquid capital to give you a better quality of life in your retirement.

If you do decide to make a move then there are also a few important points to consider:

- Will the property be easy to convert as your needs change with age?
- Is the area that you are moving to convenient in terms of amenities, doctors, hospitals etc?
- Is the area quiet in the daytime or is it noisy?
- Is the property secure?

It may well be worth doing an analysis of the good and bad points of your current home before making any decision. Of course, it may well be that, notwithstanding the good points of your current home, it is simply too large to continue to occupy, too expensive and a move is essential.

When making your decision, it is well worth looking at Housing Options for Older People (HOOP) which is a self-assessment form for people wondering whether to move. The form is available from the Elderly Accommodation Council (see useful addresses)

Moving to retirement housing

Retirement housing falls into several categories depending on need. It is usually available for those over 60, although there are a number of schemes which are designed for the over 55's. These schemes usually comprise of a number of flats, some with a resident warden, most with an alarm system connected to a central base which can summon help in the event of an emergency. There are many different types of scheme. You basically get what you pay for and those with a number of services will have a corresponding service charge to match.

Many schemes will have a communal laundry and also, in some cases, a kitchen and dining room where meals can be purchased. A guest room is also usually available.

You may decide that sheltered housing (as it is usually referred to) is the ideal choice for you. The presence of a scheme manager might be reassuring and the company of others in a communal area may suit you. However, before deciding on this option, you need to weigh up the advantages and disadvantages of more sheltered housing. There will be the feeling of being 'herded' together and the loss of independence. If you feel like this you should also see whether you can receive the range of services offered in sheltered housing in your own home.

Renting retirement housing

Most retirement homes for rent are provided by local authorities and housing associations, although not all. There are also a number of schemes offered by the larger private providers although they have to manage to high standards set by local authorities. The Elderly Accommodation Counsel can offer advice (see useful addresses).

Purchasing a retirement home

Retirement housing for sale is usually constructed by private developers although an increasing number of housing associations are also providing this type of accommodation now. Once all the properties in a scheme have been sold then the management of the scheme will be handed over to a private management company or housing association. The management organisation will be responsible for the overall management and service provision. Most retirement homes are sold on a leasehold basis with an annual ground rent (typically £250 per annum) and with a service charge that will depend on what services you are being provided. These can range from skeletal to intensive depending on your requirements.

When purchasing a retirement home it is always wise to buy off a developer who is registered with the National House Building Council (NHBC). The NHBC has a code of practice applying to all retirement homes built after 1ˢᵗ April 1990. If you are seriously considering buying into, or renting retirement housing there are a number of important points to consider:

- As with all housing, is the property in a convenient location and will it cater for your needs when you get older?
- What are the facilities within the scheme?
- Will the new property take your existing furniture or will you have to sell this and buy new?
- Most important, are the managing agents experienced in managing retirement housing?
- Who runs the management association, will leaseholders have a say in running it?
- How much is the service charge and what does it cover?
- What are the other expenses involved?
- If there is a separate sinking fund for future major repairs how do residents contribute to it?
- What are the arrangements for resale?
- Does the lease cover what will happen if your health deteriorates whilst you are in the property?
- Who owns the freehold of the property?

The above questions should be answered by the information provided in the Purchasers Information Pack which must be provided. The NHBC Code of Practice sets out what information should be in the pack.

Although many basic rights of leaseholders have been developed over the years and are enshrined in law, the lease is still paramount in terms of what services you will receive, how they are provided and what they will cost.

Invaluable advice for those living in, or intending to move into, retirement housing is provided by AIMS (Advice, Information and Mediation Service for Retirement Housing) See useful addresses. AIMS provides useful written information, prepared in conjunction with LEASE (the Leasehold Advisory Service) called Leasehold Retirement Housing, Your Rights and Remedies.

Options for people with limited resources

Most retirement housing is sold, as with other housing, at full market value. It follows that when you sell you get the current market value. When you sell your own property and look for retirement housing, you might find yourself in a position of not being able to buy elsewhere. This has particularly been the case in the last few years of spiralling house prices and the general distortions of the British housing scene. If you are in the position of not being able to buy elsewhere after selling your home, there are a few options to consider.

Shared ownership housing

Some housing associations and, increasingly due to over-development, private developers, run schemes where you can part buy and part-rent. There are all sorts of names used to describe this model, such as homebuy, but essentially it is what it always has been, shared ownership. In this case, you buy a percentage of the value of the property, say 25%, and then you rent the other 75%. On top of this there will be a service charge (with flats and some houses). It is not the cheapest way to obtain housing but it ensures that you get your foot on the property ladder. You should make enquiries of your local housing association which will point you in the right direction.

Lifetime lease

Some companies offer a lifetime lease, or occupancy, which means that you buy the right to live in your home for the rest of your life. The properties are sold below the market price but you will probably get very little back if you need to move again. They are also known as life interest plans.

To find out if there are any schemes in your area you should contact your local council or the Elderly Accommodation Council (address at back of this book).

Moving to rented accommodation

If you wish to move home but cannot afford to buy elsewhere, then renting privately is another option. Rented accommodation is provided in the main by local authorities, housing associations and the private sector. It is easier to rent privately than through the public sector as there is quite often a long waiting list for property and your capital may rule you out. However, tenancies in the private sector are usually insecure in that they are let out on assured shorthold tenancies which usually have a fixed duration of six months. If you wish to rent privately you should always try to go for a minimum term of twelve months. Property investors who are holding onto property for a longer term will usually be willing to do this as they are always on the lookout for a good tenant who will pay their rent. Beware of lettings agents who will let the property for six months and then charge you for another six month let. This is an old scam and you should always ask about renewal charges.

Options for existing public sector tenants

If you are already a local authority or housing association tenant, and wish to relocate to another area, you may be able to exchange your home with another council or association tenant. This will be dependant on whether the exchange is suitable, taking into account the size of the respective properties or whether any possession orders or rent arrears exist. The council or association cannot unreasonably refuse the exchange. You will find details of exchange schemes at your local council or by making enquiries to your local housing association. The Internet also has details of several national exchange schemes.

Right to buy

If you have been a council tenant for five years or more you will usually have the right to purchase your property at a discount. The discounts are not as generous as they used to be and will vary from council to council. You won't usually be entitled to buy your home if you are a housing association tenant, although there are some exceptions such as stock transfers from local authorities to associations where the right to buy is preserved. You won't, however, be able to exercise the right to buy in housing that is exclusively reserved for elderly people.

Moving to specialist housing

People who are finding it difficult to manage on their own may prefer to move to some sort of specialist housing. In addition to retirement or sheltered housing which has been outlined, there are various types of special housing to suit differing needs.

Extra care retirement housing

Some local councils and housing associations provide sheltered housing that provides extra levels of care. This housing is for people who need personal care services, such as help with dressing or bathing. This accommodation is usually provided in flats and there will normally be a shared lounge and dining rooms where meals are available. Housing in this category is usually run jointly with local authorities and people are placed there after a social services assessment. For more information on such schemes you should contact the Elderly Accommodation Council

Almshouses

Almshouses are run by charitable trusts and in turn provide accommodation for older people. Each charity will have its own rules about the types of people that they house. A few almshouses can provide extra care for vulnerable residents. Residents, as the beneficiaries of charity, do not have the same legal rights as other tenants. The individuals rights will be outlined in a 'letter of appointment' provided by the trustees or the clerk to the trustees. For more information on Almshouses, contacts the Almshouses Association, address at the back of this book.

Abbeyfield houses

Abbeyfield provides housing for people in need of sheltered accommodation. Usually this will consist of unfurnished bedsits with shared lounges, dining rooms and a shared garden. The weekly charge will include two meals a day, prepared by a resident housekeeper and also facilities for residents to prepare their own breakfasts and also snacks during the day. Typically, an Abbeyfield resident will be over 75 who is supported by a network of local volunteers. Further details can be obtained from the Abbeyfield Society address at the back of the book.

Housing for those with a disability

Many councils and associations have properties which have been specially designed for people with disabilities. This is referred to as mobility or wheelchair housing. In addition, grants are available for converting existing with disabled access. Councils and housing associations also now build what is known as lifetime homes which are designed to be adapted to peoples needs as they get older.

Living with a relative

If you are thinking of moving in with a relative, or a friend, or if you are thinking of having an older relative live with you, you should always weigh up the pros and the cons of such a move. Some of the things to consider are:

- How well will you get on with the person under the same roof?
- Is there enough space?
- Will a downstairs bedroom be needed?
- Is the housing conveniently situated?
- What are the financial arrangements?
- What are the practical arrangements, such as cooking and washing?
- What would be the implications if you or your relative needed extra care?

You should also speak to your local benefits office about the implications for benefits received when you have made the move.

Moving abroad

Many people dream of leaving the UK and moving to a warmer climate when they have retired. However, the financial climate has changed significantly in the last few years and thorough research is necessary before contemplating such a move. Many people have moved away, particularly to places like Spain, and have returned after a few years, either disillusioned or lonely or having lost money on a property that they have purchased.

It is fairly easy to make enquiries about residency requirements in the various countries. The Foreign and Commonwealth office can provide information and contact details for the relevant consulates or embassies in the various countries. However, before even contemplating such a move, there are various questions that you need to address:

- Can you afford to move to another country? You have to be very clear about your financial situation in retirement. House prices abroad may seem cheap compared to the UK. However, the process of buying can be complicated and some countries, such as Spain, can be problematic. In addition, there has been a collapse in the housing market in Spain due to over development. Caution is advised. You will need to have enough surplus income to live as well so careful planning is needed.

- You will need to think about pension rights and health costs abroad.

- What about possessions? You will need specialist advice about furniture and so on, and the costs of moving.

- Can you take pets? You should always ask a vet's advice first. The Pet Travel Scheme (PETS) allows dogs and cats to re-enter the UK from certain countries without quarantine as long as they meet certain conditions. You can get further information from the Department for Environment, Food and Rural Affairs' PETS Helpline (see back of book).

- Will you want to find work? You will need professional advice about work permits in the respective countries.

Buying a property abroad

There are property magazines covering homes for sale or rent. Also, property developers are represented at retirement exhibitions. However, a word of caution, you will certainly need professional advice before embarking on a property purchase. It might be useful to buy a book on purchasing a property abroad. You will find case studies of people who have bought successfully and others who have had bad experience. For certain you will need to do your homework well. One useful tip is to ensure that a local agent selling property is working within the rules set by FOPDAC, (The Federation of

Overseas Property Developers, Agents and Consultants: www.fopdac.com)

There are also UK firms of solicitors who specialise in the purchase of property abroad. Addresses for such solicitors can typically be found on the Internet.

Repairs and Improvements

One of the most important elements of your home is that of its condition. When you retire or are close to retiring, this presents the ideal opportunity to assess the overall condition of your home and to draw up a condition survey (or have one drawn up) so that you can plan expenditure. It is wise to commence the work as soon as possible after retirement, or before if possible, so that you can still carry out works yourself, without resorting to using building firms. This will save money and mean that you have more control. This chapter also points the way to the various agencies that exist which will give you advice on repairs and maintenance and also funding.

Deciding what needs to be carried out

There are specialist advice agencies, called Home Improvement Agencies (sometimes called Care and Repair or Staying Put) that will give specialist advice to older and vulnerable householders and also to people living in private rented accommodation. They are small scale, not-for-profit organisations, usually managed locally by housing associations, councils or charities. They will usually offer practical help with tasks such as arranging a condition survey, getting estimates from builders (trusted builders) applying for grants or loans and also keeping an eye on the progress of work. They may charge a fee towards their assistance, which is usually included in the grant or loans that you may be in receipt of.

To find out whether there is a home improvement agency in your area, you should contact your local Age Concern or the local council housing department or Foundations (the National Co-ordinating Body for Home Improvement Agencies) address at the rear of the book.

If there is no Home Improvement Agency in your area you might want to engage a surveyor to carry one out for you. As these are costly, or can be, you should always ask what the cost will be first. The Chartered Surveyor Voluntary Service exists to help people who would other wise be able to get professional advice. You need to be referred to them by a Citizens Advice Bureau first.

Finding a Builder

If there is no Home Improvement Agency in your area, you should take care, great care, when trying to find a good reliable builder. We have all heard stories of rogue builders who carry out shoddy work and charge over the odds. If you intend to employ a builder, particularly for a larger job, then you should always employ a builder backed by a proper guarantee scheme. The Federation of Master Builders (FMB) offers a MasterBond Warranty: its members must meet certain criteria and adhere to the FMB's Code of Practice. The ten-year insurance backed warranty will add 1.5% to the total cost of a job but is money well spent.

Information on this scheme can be obtained from the FMB website at www.fmb.org.uk.

To ensure that you get a good job done, the FMB recommends that you:

- Always ask for references and names of previous clients
- Get estimates from two or three builders
- Ask for the work to be covered by an insurance backed warranty
- Get a written specification and quotation
- Use a contract (the FMB has a plain English contract for small works)
- Agree any staged and final payments before a job

- Avoid dealing in cash

The FMB has played a leading role in the development of the government backed TrustMark scheme, which is a consumer protection initiative for the home repair and improvement sector. A wide range of traders, including plumbers and electricians, are being licensed to become TrustMark registered firms. For more information contact TrustMark address at the rear of this book.

Financial help with repairs and improvements

Sometimes, individuals find themselves in a position where they cannot afford repairs to their homes. There are, however, various forms of assistance at hand. Local authorities have general powers to provide help with repairs and also adaptations to housing. The assistance isn't always cash based, it can also be provided in the form of labour material or advice. The cash element will usually be either grants or loans. Local authorities will have published policies explaining the various forms of assistance. These can vary from time to time, as many of them are dependant on national legislation and government funding. Below are a few of the types of grants available.

Disabled facilities grant

These grants provide facilities and adaptations to help a disabled person to live as independently and in as much comfort as possible. They are means tested, i.e. dependant on income, with the exception of grants for disabled children. In its assessment, the council will take into account only your income and that of your partner or spouse. If you receive the guarantee part of Pension Credit, Income Support or income based Jobseeker's allowance you will not normally have to make any contribution. People receiving Working or Child Tax Credit (with gross taxable income of less than £15,000) have these payments disregarded as income. The grant is usually mandatory provided that your home needs adaptations to enable you to use essential facilities such as kitchen or bathroom. The maximum amount of grant is £30,000. You can get more information about these grants from your local authority housing department.

If you receive Pension credit, Income Support or Income based jobseekers allowance, you may be able to get a Community care Grant or Budgeting Loan from the Social fund to help you with the cost of minor repairs.

Social services departments provide funding for some minor adaptation works. They may also be able to help with some types of work not covered by the disabled facilities grant.

If you want to raise capital from your home to pay for works, the Home Improvement Trust may be able to help. It is a not-for-profit company that has links with a number of commercial lenders who provide older people with low cost loans raised against the value of their home. You can contact Home Improvement Trust direct at the address at the rear of the book.

The Care and Repair England publication also provides useful information about organising and financing building works. You can get a copy by phoning 0115 950 6500 or by downloading it from the website www.careandrepair-england.org.uk.

Adapting your home

You may need to make certain adaptations to your home if you or a member of your family needs them, such as mobility aids, to make it easier to navigate the house. There are other areas that can be helpful, such as the positioning of the furniture. Occupational Therapists can give detailed advice. They can assess a person's mobility and their ability to move around and can provide appropriate advice. You should contact your local social services department and ask for an assessment of needs. You don't have to have a letter from the doctor but this can speed things up. Social services should provide some equipment free if you or a relative is assessed as needing them. All minor adaptations costing less than £1000 must be provided free of charge.

For full information about special equipment and furniture, contact the Disabled Living Foundation at the address at the rear of the book.

5

Raising Capital from your Home

Equity release schemes
The main principle behind equity release schemes, which enable you to release cash from your home, is that you are offered a lump sum or an income now but you, or your estate, have to pay back a larger sum to compensate the investors (the Equity release companies). This amounts to a longer-term loan which is paid back later with rolled up interest. If you wish to raise money but do not wish to move home then these schemes could be for you.

Equity release schemes come in two basic forms: lifetime mortgages and home reversion schemes.

Lifetime mortgages
With a lifetime mortgage you borrow against the value of your home but the capital, and usually the interest are repaid only on your death or when you move out. Lifetime mortgages can be taken out jointly with your spouse or partner, in which case the loan does not have to be repaid until the second death. You can use a lifetime mortgage to raise a single large cash sum. If you want an income you can draw out a series of smaller sums or use a single lump sum to buy an investment, such as an annuity. The former is more tax efficient because the income from an annuity is usually taxable.

Types of lifetime mortgages
With the most common form of lifetime loan-a roll up loan-interest is added each month to the amount that you owe. You are charged interest not just on the amount that you originally borrowed, but to the increasing balance as interest is added. The interest can be fixed

for the whole life of the loan or can be variable. When your home is eventually sold, the proceeds are used to repay the outstanding loan and what is left over goes to your estate. Different providers set different age limits but you must be at least 55 or 60 with most schemes to be eligible for a lifetime mortgage. In addition, the value of your home, less any debts secured against it must be in the region of £50,000 and upwards. If you have an existing mortgage you will usually be required to pay this off with the loan. The amounts that you can borrow will vary with your age. The maximum for a roll up loan is usually about half the value.

Reversion schemes

With a reversion scheme you sell part, or all, of your home, but retain the right to live there either rent free or for a token rent. When the home is eventually sold, the reversionary company takes a percentage of the sale proceeds, or the whole amount if you sold 100 per cent of your home. This means that the reversion company, as opposed to the estate gets the benefit of any increase in value of your home. A reversion scheme can be taken out singly or jointly, in which case it continues until the second death.

As with lifetime mortgages, reversion schemes can pay you a single lump sum or a series of smaller lump sums. Alternatively, they may be combined with an annuity or other investment to provide you with a regular income. Investment income is usually taxable but lump sums from the sale of your home are not. The money that you get when you take out the loan will be smaller than the value of the part of your home that you sell. This difference represents the return to the reversionary company. A key factor that the reversionary company uses in deciding what it will offer is how long it expects to have to wait before it gets its money back. To qualify for a reversionary scheme you will usually be between 65-70. Your home must be in reasonable condition and worth a minimum amount, typically £75,000.

Alternatives to equity release

One of the most common reasons for considering equity release is to raise extra income for day-to-day living. If this is your main motive, you might want to consider ensuring that the other avenues for raising income have been explored. For example:

- Are you claiming all the state benefits due to you, such as Pension Credit, Council Tax Benefit and Attendance Allowance
- Have you taken steps to trace any lost pensions that you might be claiming?
- Are you exploiting the potential of your home, for example taking in a lodger?
- Are you making sure that you are not overspending?
- Are you paying too much tax?

You cannot normally use equity release to raise a lump sum of below £10,000. If such a sum is needed you might want to consider taking out an interest only mortgage. Unlike a lifetime mortgage you pay interest each month so the amount borrowed does not grow.

The main thing with equity release schemes is that you should get good advice, usually independent advice so that you are totally aware of what it is that you are signing up for.

****

6

Selling your home

As we all know, the housing market has undergone one of its periodic 'corrections' and the value of property has once again plummeted. This time it has been in the context of one of the worst recessions in living memory. Therefore, the wisdom of using your home, or factoring in your home, as a source of income when retirement age is reached, is questionable.

Falling property prices are just one of the problems if your intention is to sell up to release capital for your retirement. The other main one is that if you are aiming to downsize to a smaller home then the price of this property may not necessarily be that much cheaper than the family home that you are selling. This does depend of course on the nature, size and value of that property. In addition, there are also the other problems associated with relocating, such as getting used to a new area, neighbours and so on.

You should bear in mind as well that there are significant costs associated with selling, moving and buying. This will eat into any equity that you release from your property and should be taken into account.

The table overleaf will give you an idea of the costs involved.

	COST	EXAMPLE 1. SELLING A HOME FOR £250,000 AND BUYING FOR £150,000	EXAMPLE 2. SELLING A HOME FOR £600,000 AND BUYING FOR £250,000
AS A SELLER			
ESTATE AGENTS FEE	1.5%-2% OF SELLING PRICE	£4375	£10,500
AS A BUYER			
STAMP DUTY LAND TAX	SEE TABLE BELOW	£0	£2500
SURVEYORS FEE	APPROX £500	£500	£500
SEARCH FEES AND LAND REGISTRY FEES	APPROX £500	£500	£500
AS BOTH			
LEGAL COSTS	APPROX £1500	£1500	£1500
REMOVAL COSTS	£600	£600	£600
TOTAL		**£7475**	**£16,100**

Case study

John and Doreen

John and Doreen are selling a £350,000 family home and buying a flat for £200,000. The costs for downsizing are:

- Estate agents fees 1.5% £5250
- Stamp duty land tax 1% £2000
- Survey £500
- Search fees, Land Registry etc £500
- Legal costs on both sales and purchase £1500
- Removal costs £600

Total £10,350. The cash realised from downsizing is £350,000-£200,000-£10,350 = £139,650.

The main advantage of downsizing is that you realise the full value of the home that you are selling (apart from costs). Also, if you are selling your own home the proceeds are tax-free.

****

7

Extras because of age

Free bus travel in England for older and disabled people
Eligible older and disabled people are entitled to free off-peak travel on local buses anywhere in England. Off peak is between 9.30am to 11pm Monday to Friday and all day weekends and public holidays.

The England bus pass only covers travel in England. It doesn't give you free bus travel in Wales, Scotland or Northern Ireland.

Free bus travel in Wales, Scotland and Northern Ireland
There are similar schemes in each of the above countries and you need to apply to your respective local authorities.

Who is eligible for an older person's bus pass?
If you live in England, you will be entitled to a bus pass when you reach 'eligible age'. If you were born after 5th April 1950, the age you become eligible is tied to the changes in state pension age for women. This affects both men and women.

Women born after 5th April 1950
If you are a woman born after 5th April 1950, you will become eligible for an older persons bus pass when you reach pensionable age.

Men born after 5th April 1950
If you are a man born after 5th April 1950, you will come eligible when you reach the pensionable age of a woman born on the same day.

If you were born before 6th April 1950

You are eligible for an older person's bus pass from your 60th birthday if you were born before 6th April 1950.

Disabled persons bus pass

You are eligible for a disabled person's bus pass if you live in England and are 'eligible disabled'. This means you:

- are blind or partially sighted
- are profoundly or severely deaf
- are without speech
- have a disability, or have suffered an injury, which has a substantial and long term effect on your ability to walk
- don't have arms or have long-term loss of the use of both arms
- have a learning disability

You are also eligible disabled if your application for a driving licence would be refused under section 92 of the Road Traffic Act 1988 (physical fitness). However, you wont be eligible if you were refused because of persistent misuse of drugs or alcohol.

How to get your bus pass

In the first instance you should contact your local council (whether you live in England, Scotland, Ireland or Wales, who will tell you who issues passes in your area.

Bus passes in London-the Freedom Pass

If you are eligible disabled or of eligible age and you live in Greater London, you can apply for a Freedom Pass. This gives you free travel on the entire Transport for London network. On most services, you can use the pass at any time. You can also use your

Freedom Pass England-wide, but only during off-peak times outside of London.

If you wish to use your bus pass on coaches then you should ask the coach company about terms and conditions. For more about bus passes for elderly and disabled go to www.direct.gov.uk/en/Travel

Passport

If you were born on or before 2nd September 1929, you no longer have to pay for your passport. You can ask for a refund if you are eligible and have applied for a replacement passport since 19th May 2004.

Health

NHS Prescriptions. Once you reach age 60 you qualify for free NHS prescriptions (Currently £7.40 in 2010/11). If you are eligible you simply sign the declaration on the back of the prescription. Scotland and Northern Ireland have phased out charges for prescriptions, which became free for everyone from April 2010 (Northern Ireland) and April 201a (Scotland).

Prescriptions are already free for all in Wales.

NHS sight tests. From age 60 you also qualify for free NHS sight tests but you still have to pay for the glasses and lenses, unless your income is low. You can get free sight tests from age 40 if you are considered at risk of developing glaucoma because a close family member has this condition (or any age if you already have sight problems).

Help with bills

Winter fuel payments. This scheme is in force all over the UK and provides a cash sum to every household with one or more people over 60 in the 'qualifying week' which is the week beginning the third Monday in September. You can use the cash in any way you like. However, it is designed specifically to help you cope with Winter fuel bills. The standard payment is normally between £100-£300 depending on your situation. If you want more details concerning this payment you should go to www.directgov.co.uk.

Television licence. Anyone aged 75 or over can apply for a free television licence. It doesn't matter if there are younger people in the household but the licence must be in the name of the person aged 75 or over. If you are already a licence holder you can apply for a cheaper licence for the part year that you turn 75. The licence lasts three years at a time and you should re-apply after three years.

Your home

You can get help with heating and fuel efficiency if you are aged 60 or over.

Heating rebate over £300. This is operated under the name Warm Front in England (see useful addresses for equivalent schemes in UK). The eligibility conditions are that you are aged 60 or over, own your own home or rent privately and you have no central heating or the system you have does not work. You get a voucher/claim form to use when an approved supplier fits a new heating system. You can also get free insulation if you are 70 or over. You are entitled to free loft and cavity wall insulation under a Central Government scheme. You should check out your local authority and local energy suppliers who may also offer schemes.

Repairs and Improvements

One of the most important elements of your home is that of its condition. When you retire or are close to retiring, this presents the ideal opportunity to assess the overall condition of your home and to draw up a condition survey (or have one drawn up) so that you can plan expenditure. It is wise to commence the work as soon as possible after retirement, or before if possible, so that you can still carry out works yourself, without resorting to using building firms. This will save money and mean that you have more control. This chapter also points the way to the various agencies that exist who will give you advice on repairs and maintenance and also funding.

Deciding what needs to be carried out

There are specialist advice agencies, called Home Improvement Agencies (sometimes called Care and Repair or Staying Put) that will give specialist advice to older and vulnerable householders and also to people living in private rented accommodation. They are small scale, no-for-profit organisations, usually managed locally by housing associations, councils or charities. They will usually offer practical help with tasks such as arranging a condition survey, getting estimates from builders (trusted builders) applying for grants or loans and also keeping an eye on the progress of work. They may charge a fee towards their assistance, which is usually included in the grant or loans that you may be in receipt of.

To find out whether there is a home improvement agency in your area, you should contact your local Age Concern or the local council housing department or Foundations (the National Co-ordinating Body for Home Improvement Agencies). Address at the rear of the book.

If there is no Home Improvement Agency in your area you might want to engage a surveyor to carry one out for you. As these are costly, or can be, you should always ask what the cost will be first. The Chartered Surveyor Voluntary Service exists to help people who would other wise be able to get professional advice. You need to be referred to them by a Citizens Advice Bureau first.

Finding a Builder

If there is no Home Improvement Agency in your area, you should take care, great care, when trying to find a good reliable builder. We have all heard stories of rogue builders who carry out shoddy work and charge over the odds. If you intend to employ a builder, particularly for a larger job, then you should always employ a builder backed by a proper guarantee scheme. The Federation of Master Builders (FMB) offers a MasterBond Warranty: its members must meet certain criteria and adhere to the FMB's Code of Practice. The ten-year insurance backed warranty will add 1.5% to the total cost of a job but is money well spent.

Information on this scheme can be obtained from the FMB website at www.fmb.org.uk.

To ensure that you get a good job done, the FMB recommends that you:

- Always ask for references and names of previous clients
- Get estimates from two or three builders
- Ask for the work to be covered by an insurance backed warranty
- Get a written specification and quotation
- Use a contract (the FMB has a plain English contract for small works)

- Agree any staged and final payments before a job
- Avoid dealing in cash

The FMB has played a leading role in the development of the government backed TrustMark scheme, which is a consumer protection initiative for the home repair and improvement sector.

A wide range of traders, including plumbers and electricians, are being licensed to become TrustMark registered firms. For more information contact TrustMark. Address at the rear of this book.

Financial help with repairs and improvements

Sometimes, individuals find themselves in a position where they cannot afford repairs to their homes. There are, however, various forms of assistance at hand. Local authorities have general powers to provide help with repairs and also adaptations to housing. The assistance isn't always cash based, it can also be provided in the form of labour material or advice. The cash element will usually be either grants or loans. Local authorities will have published policies explaining the various forms of assistance. These can vary from time to time, as many of them are dependant on national legislation and government funding. Below are a few of the types of grants available.

Disabled facilities grant

These grants provide facilities and adaptations to help a disabled person to live as independently and in as much comfort as possible. They are means tested (i.e.) dependant on income, with the exception of grants for disabled children. In its assessment, the council will take into account only your income and that of your partner or spouse. If you receive the guarantee part of Pension

Credit, income Support or income based Jobseeker's allowance you will not normally have to make any contribution. People receiving Working or Child Tax Credit (with gross taxable income of less than £15,000) have these payments disregarded as income. The grant is usually mandatory provided that your home needs adaptations to enable you to use essential facilities such as kitchen or bathroom. The maximum amount of grant is £30,000.

You can get more information about these grants from your local authority housing department.

If you receive Pension credit, Income Support or Income based jobseekers allowance, you may be able to get a Community Care Grant or Budgeting Loan from the Social fund to help you with the cost of minor repairs. Social services departments provide funding for some minor adaptation works. They may also be able to help with some types of work not covered by the disabled facilities grant.

If you want to raise capital from your home to pay for works, the Home Improvement Trust may be able to help. It is a not-for-profit company that has links with a number of commercial lenders who provide older people with low cost loans raised against the value of their home. You can contact Home Improvement Trust direct at the address at the rear of the book. The Care and Repair England publication also provides useful information about organising and financing building works. You can get a copy by phoning 0115 950 6500 or by downloading it from the website www.careandrepair-england.org.uk.

Adapting your home

You may need to make certain adaptations to your home if you or a member of your family needs them, such as mobility aids, to make it easier to navigate the house. There are other areas that can be helpful, such as the positioning of the furniture. Occupational Therapists can give detailed advice. They can assess a persons mobility and their ability to move around and can provide appropriate advice. You should contact your local social services department and ask for an assessment of needs. You don't have to have a letter from the doctor but this can speed things up. Social services should provide some equipment free if you or a relative is assessed as needing them. All minor adaptations costing less than £1000 must be provided free of charge.

For full information about special equipment and furniture, contact the Disabled Living Foundation at the address at the rear of the book.

****

8

Capital Gains Tax

Some types of assets do not attract a capital gain. These are listed below. With those assets that do attract capital gains tax, the first step in working out what tax there is to pay, if any, is to take the final value, the proceeds of sale, and deduct the amount you paid, known as the initial value. However, if you give the asset away, or it was given to you, instead you will need to use the market value on the date of the gift. Also, if you began owning the asset before 31st March 1982, you can substitute the market value on that date for the actual initial value. You are allowed to deduct a number of expenses, including the following:

- Costs of buying and selling
- Costs of defending your title to the asset
- Amounts spent on the item to improve its state and enhance its value.

If the final value less initial value and allowable losses comes to less than zero you have made a loss. This must be set against any gains you make on the disposal of other assets during the same tax year. But losses that cannot be set off in this way are then carried forward for use in future tax years.

Reliefs

There is no capital gains tax on a gain or part of a gain that is covered by tax relief. The situations outlined below are common situations faced by people who are retiring:

Retiring from business

If you are self employed or run a company you will need to decide what to do with your business when you retire. There are a number of things that you can do, give the business away sell the business, shut it down.

Giving the business away

If you give the business away to an individual or a trust you and the new owner can jointly claim holdover relief from CGT. This means that any gain that you have made while owning the business is transferred to the new owner by deducting it from the initial value at which they are treated as having acquired the business. When the new owner disposes of the business, the gain is worked out using this adjusted value. Hold over relief is not given automatically and you and the new owner must make a joint claim within five years of the 31st January following the end of the tax year in which the business was transferred.

Selling your business or closing it down

If you sell your business as a going concern or shut it down and sell off the assets within the next three years you may be able to claim entrepreneurs relief. This allows you to ignore 4/9ths of any gain-in effect reducing the tax payable from 18% to 10%. However, the business gains over your whole lifetime (since 6th April 2008) on which you can claim this relief are limited to £1million. Relief is not given automatically. You must claim it within one year of 31st January following the tax year in which the business was sold or disposed of.

Selling your home

In general there is no CGT on selling your main residence. In some situations however, private residence relief might be restricted, for example if you are absent from your home for long periods or use part of your home exclusively for business or have let your home. Some periods away from home do not cause a reduction in private residence relief:

- The first year of ownership in which you might be renovating your home or rebuilding the property
- The last three years of ownership
- Periods of any length when you were working abroad
- Periods when you live in job related accommodation elsewhere
- Any other periods of absence that together add up to no more than three years as long as you lived in the home both before the first absence and after the last.

Losses

Any losses that you make on selling or giving away assets must be deducted from gains made in the same tax year. Once the gains made are reduced to zero, any remaining losses are carried forward to future years. Having deducted all your expenses, reliefs and losses you can, you next subtract your annual tax-free allowance and pay CGT at a single rate of 18% on whatever remains.

Capital Gains Tax free gains

The below are the most common gains and transactions on which you do not have to pay CGT:

- Whatever you leave on death, although Inheritance tax may be payable
- Gifts to your spouse or civil partner, provided that you live together
- Gifts to charity and local sports clubs that are eligible to be treated in the same way as charities
- Your only or main home

- Private cars
- Assets that are deemed to have a life of 50 years or less (wasting assets)
- More durable personal belongings with a personal value of less than £6000.
- Foreign currency for personal spending and British money
- Gambling and lottery wins
- Gains on certain investments, including ISA's or Child Trust Funds, Gilts and many corporate bonds.

****

9

Making a Will

It is often said that the toughest job in sales it to get people to buy fire extinguishers: no one wants to think that they and their family could be caught in a fire which could kill or injure. The same thinking seems to apply to making a will: most people in Britain have not made a will- something which their families could well come to regret.

There are two sorts of people for whom making a will is not just a good idea, but essential: Anyone who is reasonably well off or whose affairs are at all complicated, and anyone who is in a partnership. Unmarried partners (or outside a civil arrangement) cannot inherit from each other unless there is a will: your partner could end up with nothing when you die, unless they can show that they were financially dependent.

There is no such thing in England as a 'common-law marriage.'

The State moves in

When anyone dies without making a will, the law, i.e. the state, takes over. In the extreme case, where you die single and have no other surviving relatives, all your estate could end up with the Crown. And the law is not at all generous to your spouse: if you have no children, your widow or widower is entitled to the first £200,000 of assets and 50% of what remains - the rest ending up with brothers and sisters, if you have any, or with relatives you cannot remember. If there are children, the widow/widower will get £125,000, plus personal assets and income from 50% of the rest; the children will get 50% when they reach age 18 and the other

50% when the surviving parents dies. If you aim to save inheritance tax, you need to make a will. For 2009-10 the 'nil rate band' is fixed at £325,000 which means that no tax is due below that level, and anything more is taxed at 40%. How to save inheritance tax is discussed in the previous chapter but remember this: tax on the equivalent of the nil rate band is £130,000 - not chickenfeed!

How to make a will
So how do you make a will? You can draw up your own using a will-making kit which you can buy from a big stationer or download from the net. That represents the most cost-effective choice and it could work if your affairs are reasonably straightforward. But if you think that your will could be disputed, i.e. subject to legal challenge, then you need to go to a solicitor. That will be a few hundred pounds well spent and you may qualify for legal aid on financial grounds or because of age: you could ask citizens advice. You will probably know a solicitor or have employed one in a recent property deal. You will talk to friends or you can contact the Law Society for a list of solicitors near where you live.

Put yourself on paper
Before you go to your solicitor, there are two important things you need to do. Firstly, you need to put yourself on paper - everything you own that is of significant size, including cars, jewellery, property, home contents, bank accounts, shares and life insurance. At the same time, you put down all that you owe, such as mortgage, overdraft and credit card debts. You need to give precise details of the beneficiaries and be very specific about what you are leaving them.

The second thing you need to do is choose an executor, one or two people whose job is to ensure that your wishes are carried out. Your first thought may be someone younger than you (you will need their agreement to act) but there is no guarantee that they will outlive you. If no executor has been designated, the state will appoint a solicitor for you - for a fee. If you go to a solicitor, think about a formula, e.g. a partner appointed by whoever is senior partner of the firm at the time. The executors will need to know where your will is kept, with your solicitor or in your bank.

Time to revisit?

You have made your will, but you should resolve to look at it again, say every five years: people change, as do assets and liabilities. It is a good basic rule to revisit your will when a new child arrives or when you move house. Outside events can change a will: if you were single when you drew up your will, it may become invalid if you get married. But divorce or separation do not make a will invalid, so you might want to make changes. If you just want to make minor alterations, you can add supplementary changes known as codicils. These are added separately and all alterations have to be properly witnessed. If the alterations are significant, you will need to make a new will which will revoke any other wills you have made.

The case for making a will is essentially simple: as Benjamin Franklin said, death and taxes are certain, and making a will means that your family will not have to spend time and energy sorting out a complicated financial and legal set-up. But when you look beyond middle age you have to assess probabilities - you may be out of the country when your signature is needed, you may get ill or you may be injured. We are now talking power of attorney.

Power of attorney

You probably gave your solicitor a power of attorney when you sold your flat; you may have given a power of attorney to your partner when you had to go on an overseas business trip but wanted to buy some shares in the UK. A power of attorney simply gives a person the power to act for somebody else in their financial affairs or in health and personal welfare. (Rules in Scotland are different). The power of attorney you gave your solicitor was probably an ordinary power of attorney, created for a set period of time and for a specific piece of business. That all seems very practical, you may think, but why should you give anyone a power of attorney? The short answer is that if you are away or fall ill, you will need someone to look after your affairs - and that requires a power of attorney. (If this happens and you had not given a power of attorney, your friends and relatives would have to go to court, which would take time and cost money)

Ending the power
When you have given a power of attorney, there are two ways in which it can be ended. You can end it yourself by using a deed of revocation or it will end automatically if you, the donor, lose 'mental capacity.' This is where problems can arise. Suppose you gave your partner an ordinary power of attorney to handle your bank account while you go on your overseas business trip; you are mugged while on your trip and lie unconscious in hospital. Your power of attorney is ended because you are mentally out of action; for the same reason you cannot give a new power of attorney.

Your partner cannot legally access your bank account or have any involvement in your affairs: catch 22? Until last year, the answer to this puzzle was to create an Enduring Power of Attorney. Under an EPA when you were mugged on your overseas trip, your partner and/or solicitor would register with the court and they could then act on your behalf.

New EPAs cannot be created since October 2007 though any existing EPAs can be registered when that becomes necessary.

New lasting powers
EPA's have been replaced by Lasting Powers of Attorney which have separate sections for personal welfare and for property and affairs. Each of these has to be registered separately and the LP A can only

be used - similar to an EPA - once it has been registered with the Office of the Public Guardian. If you want to change your mind, you can cancel all the different Powers of Attorney, so long as you are still mentally capable. This may all sound elaborate but it represents the only answer to the situation where you cannot manage your affairs because of accident, illness, age or whatever - but someone needs to do so.

The need for a power of attorney is now that much greater because banks and financial institutions are more aware of their legal responsibilities. Formerly, a friendly bank manager might have been prepared to help your partner sort out what needed to be done while you were out of action. Now, your friendly bank manager is more likely to stick to the legal rules, if only to protect himself and his employer.

You as attorney

One of your colleagues may ask you to be his attorney; if you agree, make sure that a firm of solicitors are also involved. You will have some costs - such as when you register the power of attorney - and there are strict rules, for keeping money and property separate and for keeping accounts of any dealings for the person who gave you the power. When you register, you are obliged to tell your colleague's relatives who are free to object. This is not a job for a layman acting all by himself

10

Pensions and Planning for the Future

Planning for the future

The main principle with all pension provision is that the sooner you start saving money in a pension plan the more that you will have at retirement. The later that you leave it the less you will have or the more expensive that it will be to create a fund adequate enough for your needs.

In order to gauge your retirement needs, you will need to have a clear idea of your lifestyle, or potential lifestyle in retirement. This is not something that you can plan, or want to plan, at a younger age but the main factor is that the more that you have the easier life will be. There are two main factors which currently underpin retirement:

- Improved health and longevity-we are living longer and we have better health so therefore we are more active

- People are better off-improved state and company pensions

Sources of pension and other retirement income

Government statistics indicate that there is a huge gap between the poorest and richest pensioners in the United Kingdom. No surprise there. The difference between the richest fifth of single pensioners and the poorest fifth is about £400 per week. The riches and poorest couples is £719. The poorest fifth of pensioners in the UK are reliant mainly on state benefits whilst the wealthier groups have occupational incomes and also personal investment incomes. The tables below indicates the disparity between the riches and poorest socio-economic groups:

TYPE OF PENSIONER HOUSEHOLD

Income per week Single									Couple
				£533					£1252
			£278					£579	
		£216					£421		
	£185					£320			
£136					£225				

Poorest Next 5th Middle 5th Next 5th Richest 5th Poorest 5th Next 5th Middle 5th Next 5th Richest 5th

Source: The Pensioners Income Series 2008-2009.

Income sources of poorest and richest pensioners

Poorest	Richest
Occupational Pensions 12%	Occupational pensions 27%
Personal Pensions 3%	Personal Pensions 5%
Investment income 4%	Investment income 18%
Earnings 7%	Earnings 35%
Other 0%	Other 1%
Benefit Income 73%	Benefit Income 13%

Source: The Pensioners Income Series 2008-2009

The above illustrates that those in the poorest and wealthiest bands have a wide gap in income, in particular in the areas of earnings and investments. The richest have managed to ensure that there is enough money in the pot to cater for retirement. Those in the lower income bands rely heavily on state pensions and other benefits.

When attempting to forecast for future pension needs, there are a number of factors which need to be taken into account:

- Your income needs in retirement and how much of that income you can expect to derive from state pensions
- How much pension that any savings you have will produce

- How long you have to save for

- Projected inflation

1. Income needs in retirement

This is very much a personal decision and will be influenced by a number of factors, such as ongoing housing costs, care costs, projected lifestyle etc. The main factor is that you have enough to live on comfortably. In retirement you will probably take more holidays and want to enjoy your free time. This costs money so your future planning should take into account all your projected needs and costs. The next chapter includes a few calculations about future needs. When calculating future needs, all sources of income should be taken into account.

2. What period to save over

The obvious fact is that, the longer period that you save over the more you will build up and hence the more that you will have in retirement. As time goes on savings are compounded and the value of the pot goes up. One thing is for certain and that is if you leave it too late then you will have to put away a large slice of your income to produce a decent pension. If you plan to retire at an early age then you will need to save more to produce the same benefits. We will discuss saving arrangements further on in this book.

3. Inflation

As prices rise, so your money buys you less. This is the main effect of inflation and to maintain the same level of spending power you will need to save more as time goes on. Many forms of retirement plans will include a calculation for inflation. Currently, inflation is at a reasonable level, 2.75% per annum. However, history shows that the effects of inflation can be corrosive, having risen above 25% per annum in the past. Hopefully, this is now under control

****

11

How Much Income is needed in Retirement-Planning Ahead

For most people, retirement is a substantial part of life, probably lasting a couple of decades or more. It follows that ensuring your financial security in retirement requires some forward planning. Developing a plan calls for a general review of your current finances and careful consideration of how you can build up your savings to generate the retirement income that you need.

There are five distinct stages to planning your retirement which are summarised below.

Stage 1-this involves checking first that other aspects of your basic finances are in good shape. Planning for retirement generally means locking away your money for a long time. Once invested it is usually impossible to get pension savings back early, even if in an emergency. It is therefore essential that you have other more accessible savings available for emergencies and that you do not have any problem debts that could tip you into a financial crisis. You must then weigh up saving for retirement against other goals that are more pressing, such as making sure that your household would be financially secure if you were unable to work because of illness or the main breadwinner dies.

Stage 2-You need to decide how much income you might need when you retire. There is a table below which might help you in calculating this.

Stage 3- Check how much pension that you have built up so far.

Stage 4-Compare your amount form stage 3 with your target income from stage 2.

Stage 5-Review your progress once a year and/or if your circumstances change.

It is a fact that many people need far less in retirement than when actively working. The expenses that exist when working, such as mortgage payments, children and work related expenses do not exist when retired. The average household between 30-49 spends £473 per week and £416 between 50-64. This drops to £263 per week between 65 to 74 and even lower in later retirement (Family Expenditure Survey 2000-1).

However, as might be expected, expenditure on health care increases correspondingly with age. Whilst the state may help with some costs the individual still has to bear a high proportion of expenditure on health related items.

When calculating how much money you will need in retirement, it is useful to use a table in order to list your anticipated expenses as follows:

1. Everyday needs

Item	Annual Total £
Food and other	
Leisure (newspapers etc)	

Pets	
Clothes	
Other household items	
Gardening	
General expenses	

Home expenses

Mortgage/rent	
Service charges/repairs	
Insurance	
Council tax	
Water and other utilities	
Telephone	
TV licence other charges (satellite)	
Other expenses (home help)	

Leisure and general entertainment

Hobbies	
Eating out	
Cinema/theatre	
Holidays	
Other luxuries (smoking/drinking	

Transport

Car expenses	
Car hire	
Petrol etc	

Bus/train fares	

Health

Dental charges	
Optical expenses	
Medical insurance	
Care insurance	
Other health related expenses	

Anniversaries/birthdays etc

Children/grandchildren	
Relatives other than children	
Christmas	
Charitable donations	
Other expenses	

Savings and loans

General savings	
Saving for later retirement	
Other savings	
Loan repayments	

Other

The above should give you an idea of the amounts that you will need per annum to live well. Obviously, you should plan for a monthly income that will meet those needs. You should also take account of income tax on your retirement incomes.

The impact of inflation

When you are planning for many years ahead, it is essential to take account of the effects of inflation. Currently, in 2011, we are in a period of high inflation, largely due to sky high oil prices. As prices rise over the years, the money we will have will buy less and less. For example, in the extreme case, if prices double then a fixed amount of money will buy only half as much. The higher the rate of inflation,. The more you have to save to reach your income target.

Some pension schemes give you automatic protection against inflation, but many don't and it is largely up to you to decide what protection to build into your planning. The first step is to be aware what effect inflation might have. Fortunately, pension statements and projections these days must all be adjusted for inflation so that figures you are given are expressed in today's money. This gives you an idea of the standard of living you might expect and helps you assess the amount that you need to save.

Providers of non-pension investments (such as unit trusts and investment trusts (see later chapters) do not have to give you statements and projections adjusted for inflation. If you use these other investments for your retirement then you will have to make your own adjustments. You can do this using the table below.

Value in today's money of £1,000 you receive in the future

Average rate of inflation

Number of years until you receive the money	2.5% a year	5% a year	7.5% a year	10% a year

5	£884	£784	£697	£621
10	£781	£614	£485	£386
15	£690	£481	£338	£239
20	£610	£377	£235	£149
25	£539	£295	£164	£92
30	£477	£231	£114	£57
35	£421	£181	£80	£36
40	£372	£142	£55	£22
45	£329	£111	£39	£14
50	£291	£87	£39	£9

The above should be a good guide. If you require more detailed forecasting you can go to www.statistics.gov.uk/plc

12

Sources Of Pension Savings- Options for Retirement

1. The state pension

We will be elaborating on the state pension further in chapter 5. The state pension system is based on contributions, the payments made by an individual today funds today's pension payments and for those who are young the future contributions will foot their pension bill. Therefore, the state pension system is not a savings scheme it is a pay-as-you-go system.

Pensions are a major area of government spending and are becoming more and more so. Protecting pensions against inflationary increases have put pressure on respective governments, along with the introduction of a second tier-pension, the state second pension (S2P). This replaced SERPS. The problems of pension provision are set to increase with the numbers of older people outnumbering those in active work, leading to an imbalance in provision. The biggest dilemma facing the government, and future governments, is the problem of convincing people to save for their pensions, therefore taking some of the burden off the state.

Those most at risk in terms of retirement poverty are the lower earners, who quite often do not build up enough contributions to gain a state pension, those who contribute to a state pension but cannot save enough to contribute to a private scheme and disabled people who cannot work or carers who also cannot work. The above is not an exclusive list. The government has recognised the difficulties faced by these groups and have introduced the state second pension and pension credits.

Pension credits

Pension credits began life in October 2003. The credit is designed to top up the resources of pensioners whose income is low. The pension credit has two components: a guarantee credit and a saving credit. The guarantee credit is available to anyone over a qualifying age (equal to women's state pension age-see further on) whose income is less than a set amount called the minimum guarantee. The guarantee will bring income up to £132.60 for a single person and £202.40 for a couple (including same sex couples) (2010-2011). The minimum guarantee is higher for certain categories of disabled people and carers.

The savings credit

Pension credit also has an inbuilt incentive scheme called a savings credit which encourages people to save for their retirement.

The rules are complicated. If a person is aged 65 or over they can claim a credit of 60pence for each £1 of income that they have between two thresholds. The lower threshold is the maximum basic state pension. This is £98.40 per week for a single person and £157.25 for a couple. The upper threshold is the minimum guarantee stated above (£132.60 single and £202.40 couple). This gives a maximum savings threshold of £20.52 single and £27.09 couple (2010-11). Savings credit is reduced by 40p for each £1 of income above the minimum guarantee.

The over 80 pension

This is a non-contributory pension for people aged 80 or over with little or no state pension. If you are 80 or over, not getting or getting a reduced state pension because you have not paid enough

National Insurance contributions (NI) and are currently living in England, Scotland or Wales and have been doing so for a total of 10 years or more in any continuous period of 20 years before or after your 80th birthday, you could claim the over 80 pension. The maximum amount of the over 80 state pension that you can get is 60% of the full state pension.

2. Personal Pension Arrangements

Occupational pensions

We discuss occupational pension schemes in more depth later in this book. Briefly, occupational pension schemes are a very important source of income. They are also one of the best ways to pay into a pension scheme as the employer has to contribute a significant amount to the pot. Over the years the amounts paid into occupational pension schemes has increased significantly. Although there have been a number of incidences of occupational schemes being wound up this is relatively small and they remain a key source of retirement income.

Stakeholder schemes

Stakeholder pension schemes are designed for those people who do not have an employer, or have an employer who does not have an occupational scheme. They therefore cannot pay into an occupational scheme. If an employer does not offer an occupational scheme (many small employers are exempt) they have to arrange access to a stakeholder scheme. Employees do not have to join an occupational scheme offered by employers, instead they can join a stakeholder scheme. Likewise, self-employed people can also join a stakeholder scheme.

Stakeholder schemes have a contribution limit-this being currently £3,600 per year. Anyone who is not earning can also pay into a scheme, up to the limit above. A stakeholder pension is one form of personal pension described below.

The range of personal pensions

Personal pensions are open to anyone, in much the same way as a stakeholder scheme. These are described more fully later on in this book. Employers do not have to offer a personal pension scheme through the workplace, as they do a stakeholder scheme, though a lot do by offering a group scheme which has been separately negotiated with a provider.

Other ways to save for retirement
Other savings

The government offers certain tax advantages to encourage pension saving. However, the most advantageous savings plan is the Individual Savings Account (ISA) discussed further on in the book. In addition, you might have regular savings accounts, your home or a second home. All of these possibilities must be factored in when arriving at an adequate retirement income.

13

Women and Pensions

It is a general rule that women pensioners tend to have less income than their male counterparts. Therefore, when building a retirement plan, women need to consider what steps they and their partners can take to make their financial future more secure.

Particular issues for women

These days, the rules of any particular pension scheme-whether state or private, do not discriminate between men and women. Whether male or female you pay the same to access the same level of benefits. However, this does not always mean that women end up with the same level of pension as men. This is because of the general working and lifestyle differences between men and women, for example women are more likely to take breaks from work and take part time work so they can look after family. As a result, women are more likely to pay less into a pension fund than men.

Historically, the (idealised) role of women as carers was built into the UK pensions system. Not least the state pension system. It was assumed that women would marry before having children and rely on their husbands to provide for them financially right through to retirement. As a result, women who have already retired typically have much lower incomes than men.

Changes to the state scheme for people reaching state pension age from 6th April 2010 onwards, mean that most women will, in future, retire with similar state pensions as men. However if you are an unmarried women living with a partner you should be aware of the following:

- The state scheme recognises wives, husbands and civil partners but not unmarried partners. This means that if your unmarried partner dies before you, you would not be eligible for the state benefits that provide support for bereaved dependants.

- Occupational schemes and personal pensions typically pay survivor benefits to a bereaved partner, whether married or not. However many schemes-especially in the public sector-have recognised unmarried partners only recently and, as a result, the survivor pension for an unmarried partner may be very low.

- The legal system recognises that wives, husbands and civil partners may have a claim on retirement savings built up by the other party in the event of divorce, but these will be considered along with all the other assets to be split between you and you may end up with a much lower retirement income than you had been expecting.

- The legal system does not give similar rights to unmarried partners who split up. If your unmarried partner was building up pension savings for you both, he or she can walk away with all those savings and you have no legal claim on them.

14

The State Pension

Over 96% of single pensioners and 99% of couples receive the basic state pension. Therefore, it is here to stay. Everyone who has paid the appropriate national insurance contributions will be entitled to a state pension. If you are not working you can either receive pension credits, as discussed, or make voluntary contributions.

The basic state pension is paid at a flat rate, currently for a single person £97.65 per week. For a couple, whether married or not, who have built up their own right to claim the basic pension could receive up to twice this amount £195.30 (2010-11). A married couple can qualify for a higher pension based on the husband's NI contributions. If the wife has reached pension age her part of the pension is paid directly to her. If the wife is below pension age, the whole pension is paid directly to the husband.

Basic state pensions are increased each April in line with price inflation. State pensioners also receive a (£10 Christmas bonus-check current entitlement) and are entitled to winter fuel payments.

At the moment, only married women can claim a pension based on their spouse's NI record. This is set to change and married men who have reached 65 will be able to claim a basic state pension based on their wife's contribution record where the wife reaches state pension age on or after 6th April 2010.

Same sex couples, as a result of the Civil Partnerships Act 2004, have the same rights as heterosexual couples in all aspects of pension provision.

Qualifying for state pension

In order to receive the full basic pension, if you reach state pension age before 6th April 2010 the main rule is that you will have to have paid NI contributions for at least 90% of the tax years in your working life. If you have only paid for a quarter, for example, you may not get basic state pension. 'Working life' is defined as from the age 16 to retirement age, or the last complete tax year before retirement age. For men and women born after 5th March 1955 the working life is 49 years. For women with a pension age of 60, the working life is 44 years. The table overleaf indicates likely pension related to NI contributions. If you reach state pension age after 6th April 2010 then you will need 30 qualifying years in order to get the full state pension

State pensions related to NI contributions

Number of qualifying pension Years in your working rates Life rates	Fraction of the full Spouse/partner pension basic pension at		Your basic at 2010-2011 2010-2011
1	1/30	3.26	1.95
2	2/30	6.51	3.90
3	3/30	9.77	5.85
4	4/30	13.02	7.80
5	5/30	16.28	9.75
6	6/30	19.53	11.70

7	7/30	22.79	13.65
8	8/30	26.04	15.60
9	9/30	29.30	17.55
10	10/30	32.55	19.50
11	11/30	35.81	21.45
12	12/30	39.06	24.40
13	13/30	42.32	25.35
14	14/30	45.57	27.30
15	15/30	48.33	29.25
16	16/30	52.08	31.20
17	17/30	55.34	33.15
18	18/30	58.59	35.10
19	19/30	61.85	37.05
20	20/30	65.10	39.00
21	21/30	68.36	40.95
22	22/30	71.61	42.90
23	23/30	74.87	44.85
24	24/30	78.12	46.80
25	25/30	81.38	48.75
26	26/30	84.63	50.70
27	27/30	87.99	52.65
28	28/30	91.14	54.60
29	29/30	94.40	56.55
30 or more	30/30	97.65	58.50

For NI contributions to count towards a state pension, they must be the right type, as the table below indicates.

NI contributions counting towards a basic state pension.

See Overleaf

Type of contribution	Paid by	Details for 2010-11
No Contributions but earnings between LEL and PT	Employees	Earning between 97 and 110 per week
Class 1 full rate on earnings between PT and UAP	Employees	Earnings between 110 and 770. usually paid at 11% but less if contracted out (see further on)
Class 2	Self-employed	Flat rate of 2.40 per week. Those with earnings for the year of less than 5075 can choose to opt out
Class 3	Out of the labour market and not receiving NI credits	Flat rate of 12.05 per week

Key to abbreviations

LEL = Lower earnings limit: PT = Primary Threshold: UAP = Upper Accruals Point: UEL = Upper earnings limit. LEL, PT and UEL usually increase each year UAP is fixed. A rate is due to increase by 1% from 2011-2012 onwards.

National Insurance Contributions that do not count towards the basic state pension.

Type of contribution	Paid By	Details for 2010-11
No Contributions and earnings below the LEL	Employees	Earning less than 97

Class 1, married women's reduced rate	Employees	4.85% of earnings between 110 and 844 per week and 1% above 844 (a)
Class 1, full rate, on earnings above the UAP	Employees	11% of earnings between 770 and 844 per week and 1% on earnings above 844 (a)
No Class 2 contributions	Self-employed	Those with earnings for the year of less than 5,075 who have chosen to opt out
Class 4	Self-employed	8% of earnings for the year between 5,175 and 43,875 and 1% on earnings above 43,875 (a)

Class 1 contributions

Class 1 contributions are paid if earnings are above the primary threshold. The Threshold, set by government annually, is currently £110 per week (tax year 2010/11). If your earnings are above this set limit then you will be paying contributions at class 1 that build up to a state pension.

The level of contribution is set at 11% of earnings above the primary threshold level up to an upper earnings limit which is £844 per week in 2010/11. Contributions are paid at 1% of earnings above the upper earnings limit. If a person earns less than the primary threshold they will not pay NI contributions. The year will still count towards building up a basic state pension provided the earnings are not less than the lower earnings limit. This is £97 at 2010/11.

Class 2 contributions

Self-employed people will build up their NI contributions by paying class 2 contributions. These are paid either by direct debit or by quarterly bill at the rate of £2.40 per week (2010/11).

If profits are below the 'small earnings exception' which is £5075 in 2010/11 then there is a choice of whether or not to pay NI contributions. However, if this option is chosen, then a state pension will not be building up and there could be a loss of other benefits, such as sickness, bereavement and incapacity.

If you are a director of your own company then class 1 contributions will be paid and not class 2.

NI contribution credits

If a person is not working, in some cases they will be credited with NI contributions. This applies in the following circumstances:

- If claiming certain state benefits such as jobseekers allowance, maternity allowance or incapacity benefit
- To men and women under state pension age who have reached 60 but stopped work
- For the years in which a person has had their 16th, 17th or 18th birthday if they were still at school and were born after 5th April 1957.

If a person stays at home in order to look after children or a sick or elderly relative they might qualify for Home Responsibilities Protection. This reduces the number of years of NI contributions that are needed to qualify for a given level of pension. People who are not working and are claiming child benefit will receive Home Responsibilities Protection automatically.

Class 3 contributions

If a person is not paying class 1 or 2 contributions or receiving HRP they can pay class 3 voluntary contributions. These are charged at a flat rate of £12.05 per week (2010/11). They can be paid up to 6 years back to make up any shortfall.

National Insurance Credits

In some situations you may get National Insurance Credits, which plug what would otherwise be gaps in your NI record. You might get credits in the following situations.

- At the start of your working life. For the years in which you had your 16th, 17th and 18th birthdays if you were still at school and were born on or after 6th April 1957. You should get these credits automatically.

- While training. For the years in which you take part in an approved training course if you were born on or after 6th April 1957. Going to university does not count as an approved course. You should normally get these credits automatically.

- When you earn less than the lower earnings limit (£97 per week in 2010-11) and you are claiming working tax credit (or previously Working Families Tax Credit or Disabled person's Tax Credit) you should get these credits automatically.

- While temporarily working abroad if the UK has a reciprocal agreement with the country in which you are working and you are paying contributions there.

- While out of work because of unemployment or illness. If you are claiming job seekers allowance or Employment and

Support Allowance, you should get these credits automatically. If you are getting Statutory Sick Pay and the year in which you get it would not otherwise be a qualifying year, you need to claim this credit by writing to the NICO Contributor Group by 31st December following the end of the tax year in which you were on sick leave.

- While you are on maternity (or adoption) leave and receiving Statutory maternity or Adoption Pay and the year in which you get it would not otherwise be a qualifying year. You need to claim this credit by writing to the NICO Contributor Group by 31st December following the end of the tax year in which you were on leave.

- You are a parent of a child under the age of 12 for whom you are getting child benefit. Credits are awarded automatically. You are also eligible if you are a foster carer, but in that case you will need to claim the carer's credit.

- You are a carer looking after someone with a disability or frail through old age. You get credits automatically if you are claiming Carer's Allowance. Otherwise you will need to make a claim for the Carer's Credit.

- You are on jury service and you earnings are below a certain limit (£97 a week in 2010-11). This applies to the years from 1988-89 onwards. You need to claim this credit by writing to the NICO Contributor Group by 31st December following the end of the tax year in which you were on jury service.

- You are a man under state pension age but older than the state pension age for women. You qualify if you are not paying NI contributions or are already getting credits for some other reason. You do not have to sign on as unemployed and should get these credits automatically.

Women's state pension age is gradually increasing and when it matches the State Pension Age for men from April 2020 onwards, this type of credit will no longer be available.

The State Pension age

Currently, the state pension age is 65 for men. On 6th April 2010, the state pension age for women started to increase gradually from 60-65, to match men's. There will be further increases in the state pension age to 68 for men and women. The increase in the State Pension age is being phased in and your own particular pension age depends on when you were born. The proposed changes affect people born between April 1953 and 5th April 1960. The table below shows the proposed retirement ages. These changes are not yet law as they need to go to parliament for approval. (For your own retirement age you should go to the Pensions Service Website).

Table 1 indicates proposed pension changes for women.
Table 1.

Date of Birth	Date State pension Age Reached
6th April 1953 to 5th May 1953	6th July 2016
6th May 1953 to 6th June 1953	6th November 2016
6th June 1953 to 5th July 1953	6th March 2017
6th July 1953 to 5th August 1953	6th July 2017
6th August 1953 to 5th September 1953	6th November 2017
6th September 1953 to 5th October 1953	6th March 2018
6th October 1953 to 5th November 1953	6th July 2018

6th November 1953 to 5th December 1953	6th November 2018

Table 2 overleaf. Indicates proposed changes for men and women

Table 2.

Date of Birth	Date State Pension Age Reached
6th December 1953 to 5th January 1954	6th March 2019
6th January 1954 to 5th February 1954	6th July 2019
6th February 1954 to 5th March 1954	6th November 2019
6th March 1954 to 5th April 1954	6th March 2010
6th April 1954 to 5th April 1960	Your 66th Birthday

State pensions for people over 80

From the age of 80, all pensioners qualify for an extra 25pence per week If a person does not qualify for a basic state pension or is on a low income then they may be entitled to receive what is called ' an over-80's pension' from the age of 80.

For further advice concerning pensions either go to the government website www.thepensionsservice.gov.uk or refer to the list of useful leaflets at the back of this book.

Additional state pension

S2P replaced the State Earnings Related Pension (SERPS) in April 2002. SERPS was, essentially, a state second tier pension and it was compulsory to pay into this in order to supplement the basic state pension. There were drawbacks however, and many people fell through the net so S2P was introduced to allow other groups to contribute. S2P refined SERPS allowing the following to contribute:

- People caring for children under six and entitled to child benefit

- Carers looking after someone who is elderly or disabled, if they are entitled to carers allowance
- Certain people who are unable to work because of illness or disability, if they are entitled to long-term incapacity benefit or severe disablement allowance and they have been in the workforce for at least one-tenth of their working life

Self-employed people are excluded from S2P as are employees earning less than the lower earnings limit. Married women and widows paying class 1 contributions at the reduced rate do not build up additional state pension. S2P is an earnings related scheme. This means that people on high earnings build up more pension than those on lower earnings. However, people earning at least the lower earnings limit (£97) in 2010/11 but less than the low earnings threshold (£110) in 2010/11 are treated as if they have earnings at that level and so build up more pension than they otherwise would.

Contracting out
A person does not build up state additional pension during periods when they are contracted out. Contracting out means that a person has opted to join an occupational scheme or a personal pensions scheme or stakeholder pension. While contacted out, a person will pay lower National Insurance Contributions on part of earnings or some of the contributions paid by an employee and employer are 'rebated' and paid into the occupational pension scheme or other

pension scheme. This is discussed more fully further on in this book.

Increasing your state pension

There are a number of ways in which you can increase your State Pension, particularly if you have been presented with a pension forecast which shows lack of contributions and a diminished state pension. You can fill gaps in your pension contributions or you can defer your state pension. HM Revenue and Customs have a help line on 0845 915 5996 to check your record and to receive advice on whether you have gaps and how to fill them.

Filling gaps in your record

For people reaching State Pension Age on, or after, 6th April 2010, you need only 30 qualifying years for the full pension. Depending on your pension age your working life may be from 44 to 52 years. Therefore, under the post April 2010 rules, you can have substantial gaps in your record without any reduction in your basic pension.

If you wish to plus gaps in your contributions, normally you can go back 6 years to fill gaps in your record. However, if you will reach State Pension Age before April 5th 2015, special rules let you fill any gaps up to six years in total going back as far as 6th April 1975. You can make class 3 contributions to fill the gap, each contribution costs £12.05 so a full years worth costs 52 times 12.05 = £626.60. Making class three contributions can't increase your additional state pension. However Class 3 contributions do count towards the state bereavement benefits that your wife, husband or civil partner could claim if you were to die.

Deferring your state pension

Another way to boost your state pension is to delay its commencement. You can put off drawing your pension for as long as you like, there is no time limit. You must defer your whole pension, including any additional or graduated pensions and you earn an addition to the lump sum or a bigger cash sum.

In the past, if you put off drawing your own pension and your wife was getting a pension based on your NI record, her pension would also have to be deferred and she would have to agree to this. From 6th April 2010 onwards, husbands and civil partners as well as wives may be able to claim a pension based on their partners record. But a change to the rules now means that, if you defer your pension and your wife, husband or civil partner claims on your record, they no longer have to defer their pension as well.

If your pension has already started to be paid, you can decide to stop payments in order to earn extra pension or lump sum. But you can only defer your pension once. You can earn an increase in the pension when it does start of 1% for every five weeks you put off the pension. This is equivalent to an increase of 10.4% for each whole year.

Alternatively, if you put off claiming your pension for at least a whole year, you can earn a one-off lump sum instead of extra pension. The lump sum is taxable but only at the top rate you were paying before getting the lump sum. Whatever the size of the sum it does not mean that you move tax brackets.

The Pension Service publishes a detailed guide to deferring your State pension. See www.direct.gov.uk/prod_consum_dg/groups/dg_digitalassets/@dg/@en/@over50/documents/digitalasset/dg_180189.pdf

15

Changes to Private Pension Savings

In 2006, important changes were introduced to the way people save for their pensions. The cumulative changes over the years meant that the whole pension system had become very complex and some streamlining was needed.

The lifetime allowance

From 2006, there is a single lifetime limit on the amount of savings that a person can build up through various pension schemes and plans that are subject to tax relief. (This excludes the state pension). The lifetime allowance starts at £1.8m million in the current tax year 2010/11. The LTA will be reduced to 1.5m from 6th April 2012.

The lifetime allowance applies to savings in all types of pension schemes including occupational pensions and stakeholder schemes. There are, broadly, two types of scheme or plan:

- Defined contribution-with these types of schemes money goes in and is invested with the fund used to buy a pension. Basically, if the fund at retirement is £200,000 then £200,000 lifetime allowance has been used up

- Defined benefit-in this type of scheme, a person is promised a pension of a certain amount usually worked out on the basis of salary before retirement and the length of time that you have been in the scheme. The equation for working out lifetime benefit in this type of scheme is a little more complicated. The pension is first converted into a notional sum (the amount of money it is reckoned is needed to buy a pension of that size). The government sets out a factor that it says will be needed to make the conversion which it has said is 20. If the pension is £20,000 then this is calculated as £20,000 times £20,000 which is £400,000. Therefore £400,000 will be used up from the lifetime allowance.

The annual allowance

In addition to the lifetime allowance, there will be a lifetime allowance starting at £255,000 in 2010/11. This will fall to 50,000 for 2011/12. This is the amount that pension savings may increase each year whether through contributions paid in or to promised benefits. An addition to the promised benefits must be converted to a notional lump sum before it can be compared with the annual allowance. The government has stated that a factor of 10 should be used as a multiplier. For example, if a promised pension increases by £300, this is equivalent to a lump sum of 10 times £300 = £3,000, therefore using up £3000 of the annual allowance. The limit will be revised each year and can be obtained from the government pensions website www.thepensionsservice.gov.uk.

The annual allowance will not start in the year a person starts their pension or die. This gives a person scope to make large last-minute additions to their fund.

If at retirement the value of a pension exceeds the lifetime allowance there will be an income tax charge of 55% on the excess if it is taken as a lump sum, or 25% if it is left in the scheme to be taken as a pension, which is taxable as income.

If the increase in the value of savings in any year exceeds the annual allowance, the excess is taxed at 40%.

Limits to benefits and contributions

The present benefit and contribution limits have been scrapped. The only remaining restrictions are:

- Contributions-the maximum that can be paid in each year is either the amount equal to taxable earnings or £3,600 whichever is the greater

- Tax free lump sum-at retirement a person can take up to one quarter of the value of the total pension fund as a tax free lump sum

In the case of death before retirement, in general savings can be paid out to survivors either as an income or as a lump sum. A lump sum up to the value of the lifetime limit will be tax-free but anything over will be taxed at 55%.

If a person leaves a scheme before two years membership they can take a refund of contributions. Refunds are paid after deduction of tax at 20% on the first £10,800 and 40% on any excess.

Tax relief on contributions will either be given at source or through PAYE if relevant.

Starting a pension

With the exception of ill-health, a person must start their pension at a minimum age, currently 50 but due to rise to 55 by 2010 and maximum age 75. Schemes will administer the rules for retirement in the minimum age to 55. Special rules will safeguard the rights of people in certain occupations to retire earlier provided they had this right already on 10th December 2003, but the lifetime limit will be reduced where it is to be applied at an earlier age. The reduction will be 2.5% of the limit for every year in advance of age 55. Any unused part of the lifetime allowance can be carried forward to set against future pension earnings.

Taking a pension

Savings do not have to be converted into pension in one go. This can be staggered and pension income can be increased as a person winds down from work.

For each tranche of pension started before 75, there is a range of choices. This will depend on the rules of each individual scheme. A person can:

- Have a pension paid direct from an occupational pension scheme

- Use a pension fund to purchase an annuity to provide a pension for the rest of life

- Use part of the pension to buy a limited period annuity lasting just five years leaving the rest invested
- Opt for income drawdown which allows taking of a pension whilst leaving the rest invested. The tax-free lump sum could be taken and the rest left invested. The maximum income will be 120% of a standard annuity rate published by the Financial Services Authority. On death the remaining pension fund can be used to provide pensions for dependants or paid to survivors as a lump sum, taxed at 35%.

When a person reaches 75 years of age, they must opt for one of the following choices:

- Have a pension paid direct from an occupational scheme

- Use the pension fund to buy an annuity to provide a pension for the rest of life or

- Opt for an Alternatively Secured Pension or ASP. This is pension draw down but with the maximum income limited to 70% of the annuity rate for a 75 year old, the minimum income is nil. On death, the remaining fund can be used to provide dependants pensions or, if there are no dependants, left to a charity or absorbed into the scheme to help other people's pensions. The person(s) whose pensions are to be enhanced can be nominated by the person whose pension it is.

16

Job Related Pensions

The best way to save for retirement is through an occupational pension scheme. Employers will also contribute and pay administration costs. Schemes normally provide an additional package of benefits such as protection if you become disabled, protection for dependants and protection against inflation. Some pension schemes are related to final salary and provide a pension that equates to a proportion of salary. However, it must be said that a lot of these schemes are winding down.

Limits on your pension savings
These limits apply collectively to all private pensions (occupational schemes and personal pensions) that you may have)

Type of limit Amount	Description	
Annual contribution limit	The maximum contributions on which you can get tax relief. You can continue contributing to your 75th birthday	£3,600 or 100% of your <u>UK</u> relevant earnings for the year whichever is the greater
Annual allowance	The maximum addition to your pension savings in any one year (including for example employers	Tax year 2010/11 £255,000 but falling to 50,000 tax year 2011/12

	contributions). Anything above the limit normally triggers a tax charge, but this does not apply in the year that you start to draw the pension.	
Lifetime allowance	The cumulative value of benefits that can be drawn from your pension savings. Any amount drawn that exceeds the limits triggers a tax charge.	Tax year 2010/11 £1.8 Million falling to 1.5m from 6th April 2012.

Tax advantages of occupational schemes

The tax advantages of occupational schemes are:

- A person receives tax relief on the amount that he or she pays into the scheme

- Employers contributions count as a tax-free benefit

- Capital gains on the contributions build up tax free

- At retirement part of the pension fund can be taken as a tax-free lump sum. The rest is taken as a taxable pension

People aged 65 and over receive more generous tax allowances than younger people. Tax allowances are dealt with further on in the book.

Qualifying to join an occupational scheme

An occupational scheme can be either open to all or restricted to certain groups, i.e. different schemes for different groups. Schemes are not allowed to discriminate in terms of race or gender or any other criteria. Employees do not have to join a scheme and can leave when they wish. There might however be restrictions on rejoining or joining a scheme later on. Not all employers offer an occupational scheme. Another pension arrangement such as a stakeholder scheme or Group Pension Scheme might be offered.

The amount of pension that a person receives from an occupational scheme will depend in part on the type of scheme that it is. Currently, there are two main types:

- Defined benefit schemes, promising a given level of benefit on retirement, usually final salary schemes

- Money purchase schemes (defined contribution schemes), where a person builds up their own savings pot. There are hybrid schemes where both the above are on offer but these are not common.

Final salary schemes

With final salary schemes, a person is promised (but not guaranteed) a certain level of pension and other benefits related to earnings. This is independent of what is paid into the scheme. Final salary schemes work well when a person stays with their employer for a long length of time or work in the public sector.

A person in such a scheme will typically pay around 5% of their salary into the scheme with the employer paying the balance of the cost which will be around 10% of salary on average. When the stock market is doing well the employer is safeguarded but when the economic climate is changing, such as at this point in time then the story is somewhat different and the employer has to pay more to maintain the level of pension. This is why such pension schemes are being withdrawn.

The pension received at retirement is based on a formula and related to final salary and years of membership in the scheme. The maximum usually builds up over 40 years. The accrual rate in such a scheme is one sixtieth or one eightieth of salary per year in the scheme.

If a person leaves the pension scheme before retirement they are still entitled to receive a pension from the scheme, based on contributions.

'Final salary' defined

The final salary is defined in the rules of the scheme. It can have a variety of meanings, for example average pay over a number of years, average of the best salary for a number of years out of ten, or earnings on a specified date. What counts are the pensionable earnings, which may mean basic salary, or could include other elements such as overtime, bonus etc.

A lump sum tax-free is included in the scheme which is defined by HMRC rules. The lump sum after 40 years of service will be around 1.5 times the annual salary.

Money purchase schemes

Money purchase pension schemes are like any other forms of savings or investment. Money is paid in and grows in value and the proceeds eventually provide a pension. The scheme is straightforward and has its upsides and downsides. The upside is that it is simple and portable. The downside is that it is related to the growth of the economy and can shrink as well as grow.

It is more difficult to plan for retirement with this kind of scheme, as distinct from the final salary scheme. As we have seen, employers prefer this kind of scheme because, although they pay into it, it doesn't place any onerous responsibilities on them.

The pension that is received on retirement will depend on the amount paid into the scheme, charges deducted for management of the scheme, how well the investment grows and the rate, called the annuity rate, at which the fund can be converted into pension. A major problem for pension schemes has been the decline in annuity rates in recent years.

With most money purchase schemes the proceeds are usually given to an insurer who will administer the funds. The trustees of the scheme will choose the insurer, in most cases. In some cases, contributors are given the choice of investment. This choice will usually include:

- A with-profits basis which is a medium-risk option and which is safer and more likely to provide a good return if a person remains with the same employer. The value of the fund cannot fall and will grow steadily as reversionary bonuses are added. On retirement a person will receive a terminal bonus, which represents a chunk of the overall return

- A unit linked fund- where money is invested in one or more funds, e.g. shares, property, gilts and so on.

The cash balance scheme

A cash balance scheme lies somewhere between a final salary scheme and a money purchase scheme. Whereas in a final salary scheme a person is promised a certain level of pension at retirement with a cash balance scheme a person is promised a certain amount of money with which to buy a pension. The amount of cash can be expressed in a number of ways, for example as a percentage of salary per annum for each year of membership. So if a person is earning £50,000 per annum and the cash balance scheme is promising 15% of salary for each year of membership, there would be a pension fund of £50,000 times 15% which equals £75,000 after 10 years of membership.

Tax

Whichever type of pension that is offered, the government sets limits on maximum amounts that a person can receive. HMRC sets limits on occupational schemes which relate mainly to final salary schemes and which are shown below.

Main HMRC limits on pensions.

1. If you are in a scheme set up on or after 14th March 1989 or a scheme set up before 14th March 1989 but you joined on or after 1st June 1989, or are in a scheme set up before 14th March 1989 which you joined on or after 17th March 1987 but before 1st June 1989 if you elected to be treated under the 'post 1989 regime'.

Under the above rules you will get a percentage of final salary up to £68,000 with a limit on the lump sum at retirement of 1.5 times final salary up to a maximum of £150,000. These are the limits for the current tax year.

2. If you are in a scheme set up before 14th March 1989 which was joined on or after 17th March 1987 and before 1st June 1989 you will receive a percentage of final salary up to a maximum of 1.5 times salary or £150,000.

If you joined a scheme before 17th March 1987 you will receive a percentage of final salary up to 1.5 times salary.

Normally, the maximum pension and any other benefits build up over a long period, usually 40 years. The pension builds up at a rate of one sixtieth of final salary for each year that you are with the employer. The maximum lump sum builds up at a rate of three-eightieths of final salary.
The rules allow for a faster build up of pension if a person can't build up pension over such a long period.

The pension scheme will set a pension age, and although there used to be difference in the age at which pension was paid to men and women respectively, the dates are now usually harmonised. The most popular age for receiving pension is 65 although some opt for 60. The lowest age at which pensions can be paid is 50. In most cases, a person must give up a job before receiving an occupational pension from an employer. The rules are in the process of changing so that a pension can be received from an employer whilst still working for that employer.

Tax rules set a limit on the amount that a pension can be increased each year. This is usually inflation. If the starting pension is less than the Inland Revenue maximum then bigger increases are allowed. For pensions built up from April 6th 1997 onwards the increase is limited to a limited price indexation which means that each year the pension can be increased in line with inflation up to a maximum of 2.5% per year.

Contributions into occupational schemes

Some occupational schemes are non-contributory, which means that the employer pays all contributions. The majority of schemes, however, are contributory, with the employer and employee contributing. Usually, the employee will pay 5% of salary. With money purchase schemes the employer will also pay a specified amount of salary. With final salary schemes, which as stated are becoming less and less common, the employer will make up the balance needed to provide the specified amount.

Both employer and employee will get tax relief on contributions.

Top-up schemes exist which can be used to top up pension pots but these are liable for tax in the usual way. There are two main types of top-up scheme:

- Unfunded schemes. With these schemes, an employer simply pays benefits at the time that a person reaches retirement. Income tax will be due on any benefits, even on lump sums

- funded schemes (Funded Unapproved Retirement Benefit Schemes or FURBS). This is where the employer pays contributions which build up funds to provide the eventual benefits. At the time that contributions are made they count as tax-liable fringe benefits. Usually the fund is arranged as a trust, which attracts only normal rates of tax. The benefits are tax-free when they are paid out, having been subject to tax.

If an employer runs a scheme which a person is eligible to join they must be given information about it automatically. The rules are as follows:

- an explanatory booklet must be given within two months of commencing employment if eligible to join, or within 13 weeks of joining

- each year a summary trustees report an annual accounts must be given

- employees can request a copy of the full accounts which must be provided on request

- an annual benefit statement must be provided

- options on leaving the scheme and benefit entitlements, transfer value must be provided within 3 months of request

- any announcements of changes to the scheme must be given to the scheme member within one month of the change being made

17

Group Personal Pension Schemes

Group personal pension schemes are a popular alternative to occupational pension schemes, particularly to smaller employers.

Group personal pension schemes are not occupational pension schemes. They are pension schemes tailored to employees of a company. The employer is not obliged to pay anything into such schemes, although many do. The amount an employer will pay is often less than an occupational pension scheme. The employee will usually end up contributing more.

Group personal pension schemes work on a money purchase basis, and, as we have seen, the employee will bear all the risks themselves. The administration charges for group personal pension schemes are usually the same as other pension funds. A plus side of group schemes is that they are seen to be particularly suitable for employees on short term contracts who cannot build up reasonable benefits in an occupational scheme because of frequent job changes. Group pension schemes are personal and travel with the employee and can be kept going without a break.

Group Personal pension Schemes and stakeholder schemes

Since October 2001, employers with more than five employees must offer at least an occupational pension scheme, a group scheme or a stakeholder scheme to employees. Stakeholder schemes are outlined further on in the book. The pension on retirement from a group scheme will depend on the same factors as all money purchase schemes, such as the overall amount paid in and the performance of the investment. In addition, the charges taken to administer the scheme will influence the amount left in the pot.

In terms of receipt of a tax-free lump sum, group schemes are exactly the same as all other pension funds.

****

18

Contracting Out Through Occupational Schemes

Employees who are building up a state additional pension can contract out, which means that a person gives up their additional state pension and instead builds up a replacement through an occupational scheme or a personal pension scheme.

Contracting out essentially means that a person receives less pension at retirement from the state. Because this saves the state money then it pays back part of the NI contributions that the employee and employer are paying now. These repayments are invested in the personal or occupational scheme to raise its value. Contracting out has not benefited everyone and how much it benefits an individual depends on how much is given up on the value of the additional state pension. This in turn depends very much on the type of scheme that is used to contract out. Although in many cases, an individual has the choice whether or not to contract out, if an employee belongs to a contracted out fund then the choice has already been made. The only way to rejoin S2P would be to leave the scheme.

How contracting out operates in an occupational scheme
As stated, if a person is contracted out in an occupational pension scheme, then both employee and employer will pay lower NI contributions which are reinvested in the scheme.

Contracting out before 6th April 1997
During the period between 6th April 1978 and 6th April 1997, contracting out meant giving up the State Earnings Related Pension

(SERPS). For pension rights built up over the period up to 6th April 1997, the occupational scheme guarantees to pay a minimum amount of pension at retirement, known as a Guaranteed Minimum Pension (GMP). It will also pay a guaranteed widow's or widowers pension. This Guaranteed Pension will be broadly equivalent to the amount that would have been built up in SERPS.

Contracted out final salary pension rights are different for pensions built up from 6th April 1997. A person no longer builds up any Guaranteed Pension Rights. Instead the employer must run a scheme which, for nine out of ten scheme members, is at least as good as a reference scheme which has been specified by the government. The main elements of such a reference scheme are that it must provide:

- a retirement pension at age 65 equal to one eightieth of qualifying earnings for each year of membership since April 1997, up to a maximum pension of half average earnings. Earnings to be used in the calculation are 90% of total earnings, including overtime and bonuses etc, above the lower earnings limit up to the upper limit. Earnings for the last three years before retirement or leaving the scheme are averaged. The pension must be the same for both men and women and can be paid before 65 but will be reduced.

- A widows or widowers pension equal to half the retirement pension built up if the scheme member dies either while working, after retirement or having moved on to another job while leaving the pension behind in the previous employers scheme

- Annual increases to pensions, once they start to be paid, of inflation up to 5% maximum.

Each scheme has to have a certificate from an actuary stating that its benefits are sufficient to pass the contracting out test.

Rules for contracting out from 6th April 2002

From 6th April 2002, a person contracts out of S2P instead of SERPS. As discussed, pensions provided by S2P for people on low to moderate incomes are higher than SERPS. To ensure that people still had an incentive to contract out of S2P certain rules were introduced. People earning less than the Band 3 threshold will continue to build up some residual S2P pension even though are contracted out. This means that at retirement they will get some enhanced pension through S2P.

For people earning between the lower earnings limit and the low earning threshold, their residual SERPS pension will be based on the difference between their actual earnings and the low earnings threshold. For people earning more than the low earnings threshold up to the Band 3 threshold their residual S2P will be based on the difference between the SERPS pension they would have had if SERPS had not been abolished and the S2P they would have had if they had not contracted out. There are no special rules for people above the Band 3 threshold, because for them S2P is the same as SERPS pension they would have got had SERPS not been abolished.

Contracting out through an occupational money purchase scheme

Contracting out through an occupational money purchase scheme is different. Employer and employee still both pay lower NI contributions. However, the employer scheme makes no guarantee about how much it will pay to replace the state pension. Instead the employer is required to guarantee that they will pay a set amount into the scheme that will build up the fund. The amounts invested are equal to the amounts that the employer and the employee have saved by paying lower NI contributions. The fund that is built up provides a set of benefits called 'protected rights' which comprise:

- a retirement pension which can be paid from age 60 onwards

- a pension for widow or widower if a person dies before retirement

- a pension for widow or widower if death happens if death occurs after retirement which is equal to half the pension that is received. A person can opt for a larger pension for their self with no provision for widow or widower

- increases to pensions once they start to be paid. Although this requirement may be removed.

After April 2006 up to a quarter of the pension savings can be taken as a tax-free lump sum.

Protected rights benefits build up on a money purchase basis so the amount of money that you receive as a pension will depend on:

- The amount invested

- Charges deducted from the scheme

- How well the investment does

- The rate (annuity rate) at which the pension fund can be converted into a pension.

Contracting out before 6th April 1997 and after 6th April 1997

Up to 6th April 1997 the amount of National Insurance rebate which an employer was obliged to invest for protected rights was a flat rate, the same for everyone. Where a person has built up protected rights before 6th April 1997, the DWP will work out the full SERPS pension that a person would have built up had they not contracted out. The amount built up is called the 'notional GMP' and it may be more or less than the protected rights pension that is received from the contracted out scheme. Whatever is left after subtracting the notional GMP is the amount of SERPS pension that will be received from the state.

From 1997 onwards, the rules for rebates changed. They are now age related. The older a person is the larger the rebate.

Personal pension plans

If an employer's pension scheme is not contracted out of the state scheme a person can opt to contract out on his or her own through a special personal pension called a 'rebate-only' plan. If a person belongs to a group personal pension scheme offered by an employer they will have their own personal pension plan.

Free-standing Additional Voluntary Contributions

If a person belongs to an employer scheme that is not contracted out they can contract out independently using a free-standing additional voluntary contribution scheme instead of a personal pension. However, it is usually better to take out a personal pension plan as overall the benefits are better. The DWP pays less into a contracted out AVC scheme than it does into a contracted out personal pension.

Other benefits from occupational schemes

Occupational pensions schemes, as opposed to group personal or stakeholder pension schemes, automatically provide packages of benefits. These will include:

- Lump-sum life cover and dependants pensions if death occurs before retirement

- Dependants pensions if death occurs after retirement

- Replacement income if a person has to give up work early because of ill-health or disability

- A pension if retirement occurs before normal retirement age

HM Revenue and Customs sets limits on the amounts that dependants can receive by way of pension after death.

Like the retirement pension itself, the benefits are subsidised because the employer pays some or all of the costs of provision, and a person will get tax relief on the contributions.

A widow's or widower's pension is usually paid automatically to wife or husband. partner or civil partner. Most occupational schemes usually allow the pension to be paid to someone else at the trustee's discretion. If the trustee's decide that there is no eligible person to receive it then the money remains in the scheme.

Pensions can be paid to other dependants, such as children in addition to any amount paid to a widow, widower or partner. Any one pension cannot be more than two-thirds of the maximum retirement pension that the person would have received if he or she had been alive. A pension for a dependant child ceases when that child ceases to be dependant, for example when the child reaches the age of 18, or when he or she finishes full-time education. Pensions for other dependants can continue for the rest of their lives even if they cease to be dependant.

Early retirement due to ill-health

There are no HMRC limits on the age that a person can receive a pension if they have to retire through ill-health. A person does not have to be completely incapable of work to qualify for the pension. If health is sufficiently bad to prevent a person from pursuing a normal course of work then this will qualify. However, evidence of ill-health will be needed and each scheme will set its own rules. Tax limits on the pension that is received are more generous than those that apply to retirement for other reasons. The pensions and benefits that are received cannot be more than the pension that would be received had a person worked until normal retirement age.

If a person is severely ill and not expected to live long then the pension can be converted into a lump sum. There is a tax charge of 20% on the part that could not be taken as a tax-free lump sum.

Early retirement generally

For pension schemes set up before 14th March 1989, tax rules will normally prohibit an employer pension scheme from paying a full pension before the normal retirement age for the scheme. For these schemes, the earliest retirement age allowed by HMRC is either 55 or 60, depending on when the scheme was set up and when it was joined. In practice, most schemes set their own early retirement age later than this. The most common retirement age is 65, the second most common is 60.

From 6th April 2010 the earliest retirement age is 55.

19

Leaving an Occupational Scheme

There are a number of reasons why people may want to leave an occupational scheme before retirement. One of the main ones is leaving an employer to take up another job. It could be that there is a desire to leave one pension scheme and enter another. Whatever the reason, there are a number of questions that need answering.

If a person leaves an occupational pension fund and has been a member of it for two years or more that scheme must provide a pension at retirement, called a deferred pension, or allow transfer of the contributions. A new pension scheme is not legally obliged to accept transfer.

Obtaining a refund of contributions
If a person leaves a scheme that he or she has belonged to for less than two years, there is no automatic entitlement to a refund or pension. A person can have back any contributions that they themselves paid but not their employer. Tax is paid on any refund. There may also be a deduction. A significant reduction, if a person had been contracted out of SERPS prior to April 1997 through the occupational scheme. The scheme may arrange for a person to be 'bought back into' the state scheme for the period that has been contracted out. This will cost a sum of money, called the Contribution Equivalent Premium, to the state.

For periods of contracting out after April 1997, it is no longer possible for a person to be bought back into SERPS, if membership of the scheme has been less than two years.

If a person has contracted out through a final-salary scheme and leaves, the scheme is obliged to protect contracted out pension rights. For contracted out pension rights built up before April 1997, a person is entitled to a Preserved Guaranteed Minimum Pension (GMP) and widow's or widower's pension. The amount of GMP is calculated and increased from the date that a person leaves a pension. The increase can either be in line with inflation, in line with average earnings, or by a fixed amount. GMP's can be transferred to another scheme or plan as long as that scheme or plan can be used for contracted out pension rights.

For periods of contracting out after 6th April 1997, a person can no longer build up GMPs. Instead the scheme has to provide a person with a scheme of benefits that is at least as good as those from a reference scheme. If a person leaves the scheme and leaves the benefits there then they must be increased by inflation up to a maximum each year. If a person leaves a contracted out money purchase scheme that scheme must continue to provide protected rights. Stories of people losing touch with their pensions over the years are legion and it is very important to stay in touch with the scheme and inform them of change of address and change of circumstances. There is the right to request a statement of benefits once every twelve months.

20

Transferring Pension Rights

Since 1st January 1986 anyone leaving an employer pension scheme who has a right to a preserved pension also has the right to take a transfer value instead. This is a lump sum that is judged to be equivalent to the preserved pension and any other rights given up. This cannot be received in the hand but can be transferred.

If pension rights are switched from an occupational money purchase scheme, the transfer value will quite simply be the value of that fund. If the switch is from a final salary scheme the transfer value must be worked out by an actuary. Assumptions are made about future investment growth and a lump sum to be transferred is arrived at.

If a person transfers into a money purchase scheme the sum is simply added to the fund. If it is transferred into a final salary scheme the transfer might be used to buy a fixed amount of pension at retirement, buy extra years in a fund or invested as a separate fund to be used at retirement to buy 'extra benefits' in a scheme. The pension fund that is the recipient of the fund will provide advice in this area.

Transfer to a Section 32 plan

Section 32 plans – termed buy-back bonds – are a special type of personal pension designed to accept transfer value from occupational pension schemes. The transfer value is simply transferred into the plan and used to buy a deferred annuity, which is an insurance product designed to pay out an income starting at a future date.

The decision whether to transfer from a previous employers occupational scheme has never been an easy one and many people feel that they will suffer a shortfall if they do. The benefits of transfer need to be weighed up on the basis of what information can be gathered from the new provider.

Public sector transfers can be easier as 'transfer clubs' exist. This is related to final salary schemes and allows the transfer years that have been built up to be added to the new schemes.

It is the transfer from an employer's occupational scheme to a personal pension scheme that can be problematic and where losses can occur. If the old scheme is a final salary scheme there will inevitably be loss of benefits associated with the old scheme, benefits such as transferring pension to dependants if death occurs. With occupational schemes quite often the employer will bear the cost of administration expenses whereas this will not be the case with a personal pension scheme.

Therefore, a lot of thought needs to be given to transferring into a personal pensions scheme, and as much information as possible gathered before doing so.

Winding up of occupational pension schemes

If an occupational scheme is wound up by an employer, for whatever reason, for example bankruptcy or being taken over by another firm which doesn't wish to continue the scheme, the pension entitlement from the scheme will depend on the rules of the particular scheme. Whilst some are generous others may provide only the minimum entitlement.

There are rules which make any shortfall in final salary schemes a debt of the company. Where bankruptcy occurs the debt will rank alongside that of other unsecured creditors. This is not a good position to be in as it invariably means that pensions become non-existent, although since September 2003, the position of unsecured creditors in relation to pension rights became a little stronger. There is a pecking order, as there always is in bankruptcy and the rights of those with pension funds can be obtained from the government insolvency service website. See also useful addresses at the back of this book.

21

New Duties for Employers Relating to Provision of Pensions from 2012

From 2012, changes to pensions law will affect all employers with at least one worker in the UK.

Employers will need to:

- Automatically enrol certain workers into a pension scheme

- Make contributions on their workers behalf

- Register with the Pensions Regulator

- Provide workers with information about the changes and how they will affect them.

The new employer duties will be introduced in stages over 4 years, starting in 2012. Each employer will be allocated a date from when the duties will first apply to them, know as their 'staging date'. This date is based on the number of people in an employer's PAYE scheme. Employers with the largest number of employee's in their PAYE scheme will have the earliest staging date.

These staging dates can be checked on www.tpr.gov.uk/staging.
Automatic enrolment
Workers who need to be automatically enrolled are called' eligible jobholders'. An eligible jobholder is:
- Aged between 22 and the state pension age

- Working, or ordinarily working in the UK

- Earning above a certain amount (currently proposed to be £7,475).

The location of the employer is not relevant when considering if the worker is an eligible jobholder. Neither is the worker's nationality or the length of their stay in the UK.

When considering whether a workers earnings are above or below the lower earnings limit, an employer needs to look at what is known as the workers 'qualifying earnings'. This will include earnings in salary, overtime, commission, bonuses, sick pay, maternity, paternity and adoption pay.

Choosing a pension scheme
Employers with an automatic enrolment duty will need to choose a pension scheme they can use for automatic enrolment. Information from the Pensions Regulator will be available to help inform this decision.

Employers might use an existing scheme or set up a new one with a pension provider. In addition, there is the National Employment Savings Trust (NEST). NEST is a pension scheme with the following characteristics:

- It has a public service obligation, meaning it must accept all employers who apply.

- It has been established by government to ensure that employers, including those that employ low to medium earners, can access pension savings and comply with their automatic enrolment duties.

Whether the scheme an employer uses for automatic enrolment is new or not, it must meet certain specific set out in legislation.

The scheme cannot:

- Impose barriers, such as probationary periods or age limits for workers.

- Require staff to make an active choice to join or take other action, e.g. having to sign a form or provide extra information to the scheme themselves, either prior to joining or to retain active membership of the scheme.

Each pension scheme will have its own rules, but all employers will need to provide the scheme with certain information about the person who is automatically enrolled.

Employers/employee contributions

Many employers offer a defined contribution scheme to staff. The rules of these schemes must require the employer to pay an overall minimum contribution of at least 8% of the workers qualifying earnings, of which at least 3% must be from the employer.

In most cases, government tax relief will account for 1% of the total 8%.

Employers who already have a pension scheme can confirm that it is suitable for automatic enrolment by a process called 'certification'.

Opt-out

Workers who have been automatically enrolled have the right to opt out of the employer's pension scheme by effectively giving one months notice. To opt out, workers must give notice via an 'opt out' notice to the employer. When employers receive a valid opt out notice within the 1-month period, they must pay back any contributions deducted from the workers pay.

Other workers

As well as automatically enrolling eligible jobholders, employers must also put certain other workers into a pension scheme, if these individuals ask. More information will be available from the Pensions Regulator later this year. Their website is www.thepensionsregulator.gov.uk.

22

Pensions and Benefits for Dependants

State pensions

If you die before your spouse or civil partner has reached state pension age there may be some entitlement to state bereavement benefits if you have built up the appropriate NI contributions in the years prior to your death.

The following may be available:

- Bereavement payment. This is a tax-free lump sum of £2000

- Widowed Parent's Allowance. This is a taxable income set at the same level as the basic state pension (£97.65 per week 2010-2011) plus half of any additional state pension (S2P) you had built up. The payment continues until the youngest child ceases to be dependant or until your widow, widower or civil partner, enters a new marriage or civil partnership or starts to live with someone as if they were married or registered. Your spouse or civil partner might also be able to claim Child tax credit (CTC, a means tested state benefit available to households with children).

- Bereavement allowance. This is a regular taxable payment payable to spouses and civil partners over age 45 without any dependant children. The amount increases with their age. This is payable for a maximum of 52 weeks and will cease if a spouse or civil partner remarries.

Death after retirement

If you die after you and your spouse/civil partner have both reached State Pension age

Help is given through the State pension system. Your spouse or partner, if they do not receive a full basic pension in their own right, may be able to make up the pension to the full single person's rate (£97.65 per week 2010-11) by using your contribution record. In addition, they can inherit half of any additional State Pension you had built up.

To find out more about bereavement benefits contact your local jobcentre plus, if you are of working age at www.direct.gov.uk. Advice on a full range of bereavement benefits for those who are retired can also be obtained here.

Occupational and personal schemes

Occupational and personal schemes may also offer pensions and lump sum pay-outs for your survivors when you die.

Schemes can pay pensions to your dependants (but not anyone who was not dependant or co-dependant on you) whether you die before or after you started your pension. This means your husband, wife, civil partner, children under the age of 23 or, if older, dependant on you because of physical or mental impairment. Also, anyone else financially dependant on you can benefit.

Under the tax rules, all the dependants pensions added together must not come to more than the retirement pension you would have been entitled to, but otherwise there is no limit on the amount of any one pension, although individual scheme rules may set some limits.

Dependant's pensions from occupational salary-related schemes

Subject to tax rules governing such schemes, a scheme can set its own rules about how much pension it will provide for dependants. Typically, a scheme will provide a pension for a widow, widower, civil partner or unmarried partner on:

- death before you have started your pension

- death after you have started your pension.

- This will typically be half or two thirds of the pension that you were entitled to at the time of your death. The pension must be increased in line with inflation. If you have been contracted out through a salary related pension scheme before April 1977, the scheme must pay a guaranteed minimum pension (GMP) to the person entitled equal to half the GMP's you had built up.

Lump sum death benefits

The types of lump sum that can be paid out and how they are treated for tax depends on your pension arrangement and your age at the time of death. Although the key age at which the rules change has been 75 years, this is to be relaxed and consultation is taking place. At the moment the age has now been increased to 77 and is likely to increase further following consultation.

If you die before 75, and before starting your pension, an occupational scheme or personal pension may pay out a lump sum, tax-free. This can be paid to anyone-they do not have to be your dependant. The amount paid out is tested against your lifetime allowance, as described earlier. If it comes to more than your remaining allowance, the excess sum is taxed at 55%.

If you die before 75 but have already started your pension, or an income withdrawal arrangement, or if you have reached 75 on, or after, 22nd June 2010 and you have not started your pension, the following lump sums might be available but taxed at 35%:

- Pension or annuity with a guarantee period-typically the period is five or ten years

- Annuity protection-an annuity may guarantee to pay out at least as much as its purchase price

- Income withdrawal-if you had opted for income withdrawal, the remainder of the pension fund that has not been paid out in pension can be paid on death as a lump-sum.

23

Protecting Pensions

It is not surprising that people get very disillusioned and nervous when it comes to pensions. Since the 1980's there have been a number of scandals involving blatant theft of pensions (Robert Maxwell), and also incidences of mis-selling.

During the 1950's, one of Britain's biggest insurance companies, Equitable life, offered pensions which were supposed to guarantee a fixed level of income at retirement. However, by the 1990's these guarantees became too expensive and the company could not fulfill their promises. Equitable life faced many legal challenges and stopped taking on any new business. Many pensioners found themselves with poor returns and it is only now that the government is looking at compensating the victims.

In addition to theft and bad management the usual raft of 'financial advisors' mis-sold personal pensions, taking advantage particularly of the changes in the 1980's and people confusion. Although many people received compensation, many others did not and a lot of distress was caused to a lot of people.

To add to the above a lot of companies became insolvent and there was too little in the pension funds to fulfill pension promises. In the early days (early 2000's) there was a spate of these insolvencies and lots of people lost their pension or received less than they had planned for. The government set up several schemes to help such people and a compensation scheme was set up to assist.

The main risk to pension funds lies with occupational schemes. Although people need to be aware of changes to the state pension scheme it is safe in so far as the state is unlikely to become insolvent and unable to pay. For sure people need to keep abreast of legislation and changes to state pensions but in essence the amount promised will remain safe.

Occupational schemes

As discussed above, one of the main risks to occupational pensions is that the employer might embezzle the funds. This should be difficult given the role of the pension trustees, which will be outlined below, but it is always possible. There is also the risk that the scheme cannot pay the amount promised. This can be to do with stock market fluctuations, or, as we have all painfully seen in the last few years, a deep recession which affects people and pensions globally.

Another problem that may arise is that of schemes with defined benefits, final salary schemes, changing their rules and replacing defined benefits with less generous schemes.

Protecting pensions

Occupational schemes are usually either statutory schemes or are set up under a trust. A statutory scheme is as the name implies. It is set up under an Act of Parliament and is the usual arrangement for most public sector schemes such as police, NHS, teachers and so on. Private sector schemes are usually always set up under a trust. This ensures that the scheme is kept at arms length from the employer and business, and can't go down with the sinking ship. (Many lessons have been learned post-Robert Maxwell). With a trust you will have three main elements:

- The sponsor, who will be the employer, who will initially decide on the rules of the scheme along with the benefits

- the beneficiaries, who are scheme members and any beneficiaries who might benefit if, say, a scheme member passes away

- Very importantly, the trustees who are tasked with looking after the pension fund and making sure that it is administered in accordance with the scheme rules.

The trustees are responsible for the running of the scheme but can also employ outside help, specialist help and can employ someone to administrate the scheme. They are supported in this role by the Pensions Regulator, which is the official body that regulates all worked based schemes (occupational schemes and also those personal pensions and stakeholder schemes organized through the workplace). The Pensions Regulator promotes good practice, monitors risk, investigates schemes and responds to complaints from scheme members. The Pensions Regulator has many powers, as would be expected, and can prosecute those who it thinks guilty of wrongdoing.

There is a Fraud Compensation Fund which can pay out where an occupational pension schemes assets have been embezzled or reduced because of dishonest activity. The fund is financed by a levy on all occupational pension schemes.

Other schemes

Normally, if there is a shortfall when a pension scheme is wound up, the employer would be expected to make up any shortfall. However, clearly this is not possible if the employer is insolvent and there is no money to put into a scheme. Between 1997 and 2005 some 85,000 people lost some or all of their promised pensions because of insolvency. Because of this several schemes were set up to provide protection:

- Financial Assistance Scheme (FAS). This scheme was set up and funded by the government to provide help for those pensions scheme members in greatest need where their pension scheme started to wind up between 1st January 1997 to 5th April 2005.

- Pension Protection Fund (PPF). This scheme took over from the above to provide compensation where a scheme winds up on or after 6th April 2005 with too little in the fund or an insolvent employer. In general, compensation ensures that existing pensioners carry on getting the full amount of their pension and that other scheme members get 90% of their promised pension up to a maximum limit (£29,749 at 65 in 2010-11). The PPF is financed by a levy on occupational pension schemes.

Protection of personal pensions

Nearly all personal pensions come under the umbrella of the Financial Services Authority (FSA). The FSA is a body with wide powers, given by parliament, and regulates a wide range of financial activities. In the United Kingdom, it is illegal to offer personal pensions without being authorized by the FSA. All pension providers authorized by then FSA have to go through a lot of hoops to demonstrate that they are responsible providers. The FSA oversees the activities of the Financial Services Compensation Scheme. If a firm providing personal pensions becomes insolvent the FSCS will step in and provide compensation instead. Compensation is capped at a maximum amount, which varies according to the way that your money has been invested. Currently the maximum is £50,000 for deposits, £50,000 for investments and for long term insurance (personal pensions, life insurance and annuities 90% of the claim with no upper limit).

Complaining about pensions

State pensions
In the first instance you would deal with HMRC, regarding payment of national insurance, and also the Pension Service regarding pension forecasts. You can find details about how to complain from HMRC website www.hmrc.gov.uk. If you have complained to the director of a particular office and you are not happy you can take your complaint to the Adjudicators Office (www.adjudicatorsoffice.gov.uk). This is an independent body that can deal with complaints about mistakes and delays, misleading advice and any other issue.

In the same way you should contact the Pensions Service department dealing with pension forecasts if you have a problem in this area. If the problem carries on without resolution you can contact the Pensions Service Chief Executive.

Occupational schemes
You should initially contact the pension administrator for your scheme. If the problem is not resolved at this early stage then you should say that you want to use the formal complaints procedure, which all occupational schemes must have and must provide you with details of. If you receive no satisfaction with this process then you should contact the Pensions Advisory Service (TPAS) www.pensionsadvisoryservice.org.uk.

TPAS is an independent mediation service which will help all parties reach agreement. If this doesn't work then you can go one step further and take your complaint to the Pensions Ombudsman. You must go through TPAS before the Ombudsman will consider your complaint.

Personal pensions

You should complain first to the pensions provider. As mentioned, all firms authorized by the FSA must have a formal complaints procedure. Provided that you go down this route, and you are still unhappy, then you can complain to the Financial Ombudsman Service (FOS) www.financial-ombudsman.org.uk. It will investigate your complaint and can make orders which are binding on the firm. Where appropriate the FOS can make the firm pay you up to £100,000 to put the matter right.

24

Tax and Pensions

State pensions
State retirement pensions count as income for tax purposes. Tax may have to be paid if income received is high enough. The only exception to this is the £10 Christmas bonus paid to all pensioners.

State pension is paid without deduction of tax. This is convenient for non-taxpayers. For other taxpayers, the tax due will usually be deducted from PAYE or from any other pension that is received. If the tax is not deducted it will be collected through self-assessment in January and July instalments.

Occupational schemes
A pension from an occupational scheme is treated as income for tax purposes. Usually, the pension will be paid with tax deducted through the PAYE system, along with any other tax due.

Personal pensions
A personal pension will count as income for tax purposes. The pension provider will usually deduct tax through PAYE. Likewise, any other tax due will be deducted through the PAYE system. The local tax office should be contacted in order to determine individual tax positions.

Tax in retirement
When a person retires, their tax bill continues to be worked out in the usual way. However, higher tax allowances may apply so less tax

is paid. The calculations used to work out a person's individual tax bill are as follows:

- Income from all sources is added together. This includes all income with the exception of income that is tax-free.

- Outgoings that you pay in full are deducted from taxable income. 'Outgoings' means any expenditure that qualifies for tax relief.

- Allowances are subtracted. Everyone has a personal allowance. For current allowances, contact the local HMRC Office or Citizens Advice Bureau. There is a breakdown below

- What is left is taxable income. This divided into four. The first slice 10% is paid (0-£2560) the second slice tax is paid at the basic rate (0-£35,500) the third slice 35,001-150,000 is subject to 40% tax. The fourth slice is over 150,000 subject to 50% tax. (as at 2011/2012)

- Married couples allowance-this is a reduced rate allowance, given at a rate of 10% as a reduction to a person's tax bill. Married couples allowance is given only where a husband or wife were born before 6th April 1935.

Tax allowances for retirees

In the tax year 2011/12 the basic personal allowance for most people is £7,475. However, if a person is 65 or over at any time during a tax year, there will be a higher personal allowance, the age-allowance. There are two rates of age allowance: in the 2008/9 tax year the allowance is £9940 for people reaching ages

65 to 74, and the higher age allowance is £10090 for people reaching ages 75 or more.

A husband and wife can each get a personal allowance to set against their own income. There is an extra allowance called a married couples allowance if either husband or wife, or both, were born before 6th April 1935. In 2011/12 this is £7295 if the couple are aged over 75. The allowance doesn't apply to those under 75.

While the personal allowance saves tax at the highest rate, the married couples allowance only gives tax relief at the rate of 10% in the 2011/12tax year. If the husbands income is above a certain level then the married couples allowance is reduced, but never to less than a basic amount. A wife can elect to have half the basic amount of the married couples allowance (but not any of the age-related addition) set against her own income. Alternatively, the husband and wife can elect jointly for the whole basic amount to be transferred to the wife.

Income limit for age allowance
Age allowances are reduced for people with earnings above a certain level. The personal age allowance is reduced if a person has a total income of more than £24,000 in the tax year 2011/12. The married couple's age allowance is also reduced if this is the case. In either case, the reduction is £1 for every £2 over the limit. Where the husband is receiving both age-related personal allowance and age-related married couple's allowance, his personal allowance is reduced first and then the married couple's allowance. The reduction stops once the allowances fall to a basic amount.

25

Reaching Retirement Age

On reaching retirement age, it will be necessary to ensure that all paperwork relating to pension contributions is in order. There are a number of rules that should be observed in order to ensure that any pension due is paid:

- keep all documents relating to pension rights
- start organising any pension due before retirement, this will ensure that any problems are overcome well before retirement

It is very important that communication is kept with all pension providers, and that they have accurate up-to-date records of a person's whereabouts. Each time addresses are changed this should be communicated to all pension providers. If it is impossible to track down an old employer from whom a pension is due, the Pension Schemes Registry can help. This was set up in 1990, by the government to help people trace so-called 'lost pensions'. If help is needed this can be obtained by filling in form PR4 which can be obtained from the Pensions Advisory Service or the Pensions Scheme Registry.

How to claim state pension

A letter will be sent to all retiree's about four months before retirement date. This will come from the pension service and will detail how much pension is due. The pension is not paid automatically, it has to be claimed. This can be done by phoning the Pensions Claim Line number included with the letter, or by filling in a claim form BR1. If the person is a married man and the wife is claiming based on the husbands contributions, then form BF225 should be filled in.

If the pension is to be deferred it is advisable to contact the Pensions Service in writing as soon as possible.

A late pension claim can be backdated up to twelve months. If a man is claiming for a pension for his wife based on his contributions this can only be backdated six-months.

How the pension is paid

Pensions are paid by the DWP pension direct to a bank account or Post Office Card Account. To find out more about the payment of pensions contact the DWP Direct Payment Information Line.

Leaving the country

If a person goes abroad for less than six months, they can carry on receiving pension in the normal way. If the trip is for longer then the Pension Service should be contacted and one of the following arrangements can be made to pay a pension:

- have it paid into a personal bank account while away

- arrange for it to be paid into a Post Office Card Account

- arrange for the money to be paid abroad

If a person is living outside of the UK at the time of the annual pension increase they won't qualify for the increase unless they reside in a member country of the European Union or a country with which the UK has an agreement for increasing pensions. It is very important that you check what will happen to your state pension when you move abroad. The DWP International Pension Centre can help.

Pensions from an occupational scheme

Although different schemes have different arrangements, there are similar rules for each scheme. About three months before a person reaches normal retirement age, they should contact the scheme. Either telephone or write enclosing all the details that they will need. The following questions should be asked:

- what pension is due?
- what is the lump-sum entitlement?
- how will the pension be reduced if a lump sum is taken?
- How will the pension be paid, will there be any choices as to frequency?
- Is there a widow's or widowers pension, and if so how will it affect the retirement pension?
- Are there any pensions for other dependants in the event of death?

If a person has been making Additional Voluntary Contributions, then a detailed breakdown of these will be needed.

Retiring early

Retirement earlier than the normal age for a scheme may result in payment of a pension at an earlier age. The minimum age for a pension is 50 with the exception of retirement on ill-health grounds. A scheme administrator will be able to supply full details.

Retiring late

Depending on the rules of the occupational scheme it may be possible to delay retirement and take the pension later. Again, the scheme administrators can help.

Method of payment

Depending on how the pension is arranged, it may be paid direct from the provider or via an insurance company. The usual for pension payments is either quarterly or monthly in advance into a personal bank account. The scheme administrators will be able to provide more information with regard to this.

A pension from a personal plan

In the same way as a pension from an occupational scheme, it is necessary to get in touch with the pension provider about 3-4 months before retirement date. The main questions that should be asked are:

- how much is the pension fund worth?
- how much pension will the plan provider offer?
- can an increase be arranged each year and if so how much is the increase?
- what is the maximum lump sum?
- is there a widow's or widowers or other dependants pension?
- what are the other options if any?
- can the purchase of an annuity be deferred without affecting the drawing of an income?

Pensions can only be paid by an insurance company or a friendly society so if the pension has been with any other form of provider then it has to be switched before it can be paid.

If there are protected-rights from a contracted out pension plan, these can be, may have to be, treated quite separately from the rest of a pension. Protected rights from a personal pension cannot be paid until a person has reached 60 years of age. A person must, by law, have an open market option enabling protected rights pension to be paid by another provider, if it is desired.

Choosing the right annuity

It is very important that an open market option is exercised at retirement. Advice should be obtained from a specialist annuity advisor. If husband and wife, it may be advisable to take out a joint annuity which will carry on paying out an income until the last partner dies, otherwise a widower or widow could be left in financial hardship.

One popular option is an annuity that pays a guaranteed income for five-years. The usual annuity pays a lifetime income then stops on death. Another option is to take out an increasing annuity. This is compulsory for contracted-out pension rights, but otherwise optional.

As annuities have fallen over the years, another option is to take out a with-profits annuity. This is a higher risk option but offers a higher return. Income from a with-profits annuity is usually made up of two parts: a guaranteed basic payment and bonuses. At the time of taking out the annuity a person must choose the starting income which the annuity will provide. The choice will depend on the likely level of future bonuses (assumed bonuses ABR) and the degree of risk that can be borne. There is a choice between:

- low ABR (minimum 0% or no bonuses). The annuity income will start at a very low level. But as long as any bonus is declared the income will increase.

- higher ABR (maximum say 4%). The starting income will be higher. The higher the ABR that is chosen the greater the starting income. Each year, provided the bonus that is declared is greater than the ABR that you chose, the income will increase. If the declared bonus is lower than the ABR, the income will fall back.

Annuity deferral and income withdrawal

Pension plans set up on or after 1st May 1995 can offer the option of annuity deferral and income withdrawal which allows a person to start taking an income from a pension plan but without buying an annuity. Instead, the income is drawn down direct from the pension fund. The remaining fund must be used to buy an annuity before the age of 75. The income must be reviewed every three years to ensure that the pension fund isn't being depleted too fast.

Payments of personal pensions

If the amount involved is very small then this can be taken as a lump sum. The amount is £2,500 or less or is too small to buy a £250 annuity income. Otherwise, the usual arrangements will apply, with you choosing the most convenient method of payment, by cheque, or payment monthly or quarterly into a bank account.

What happens to a company pension when you die?

What happens to your pension when you die depends on what type of scheme you have, its rules and whether you have already retired.

If you die before retirement-final salary schemes

What happens to your pension fund will depend on whether you are:

- an active member, i.e. you are still making contributions: or
- a deferred member-you have stopped making contributions (for example you have left the company) but haven't transferred your fund to another scheme.

Active members

Depending on your scheme's rules, a number of benefits may be payable, including:

- a return of all your contributions, usually repaid without interest:

- a tax free lump sum of up to four times your salary you were getting at the time of your death
- a pension for your spouse, civil partner or another dependant-often half, but as much as two thirds of the amount you would have got at pension age (as stated in the schemes rules).

These are maximum benefits, and many schemes pay lower amounts, so it's advisable to find out from your scheme administrator exactly what your scheme provides. Most schemes provide benefits for your spouse or civil partner, but if you have a partner and aren't legally married or in a civil partnership your scheme may not recognise them.

Deferred members

If you are a deferred member, your dependants often have fewer rights to benefits than if you were an active member, but again this depends on your scheme rules. You need to check with your scheme administrator.

Money purchase schemes

With money purchase schemes, the rules are generally the same whether you are an active or deferred member. Your pension fund will be refunded to your chosen beneficiary or you estate. If the scheme is contracted out of the second state pension, some of the benefit will usually be used to provide an income for your spouse or civil partner. There will often be a lump sum benefit provided by insurance cover too, but schemes vary widely and its advisable to check with your scheme administrator to find out exactly what your scheme provides.

'Expression of wish' forms

When you join a company's scheme, you will probably be asked to fill in an expression of wish form. This states who you would like any lump sum benefits to be paid to. The trustees of your scheme will usually make any final decision about who receives these benefits, but will usually follow what is said on the form. It is important to amend the form if your circumstances change.

If you die after you have retired

Most pensions have a guarantee period of five years. If you die within that time, the balance of the guarantee is paid, sometimes as a lump sum to the person who you have nominated or to your estate.

There may also be a pension payable to your husband or wife or civil partner usually for the rest of their life. It is important to check rules of the scheme as to who is entitled to receive that pension.

****

26

Continuing to Work

So far, this section has been about taking care to provide for your pension, and also when and how to draw it when the time is right. The time may not be right at the official retirement age. This is very much an individual decision and you have the right to carry on working.

Default retirement age

The default retirement age is being abolished. Before, the employer had the right to make you retire at the age of 65. However, now, if you did not receive notification of your retirement from your employer before 6ᵗʰ April 2011, the default retirement age will not apply to you. If your employer did not notify you of your retirement age before 6ᵗʰ April 2011, they can still decide at what age you retire but the reasons have to be justified to an Employment Tribunal if the decision is questioned.

Changing your job

There is nothing to stop you drawing a pension from one employer's scheme and then taking up employment elsewhere. The age discrimination rules apply to recruitment and so place a general ban on turning down an applicant on the basis of age. However, there are various exceptions. You can be turned down legally because of age if you are older than 65 (or the employers normal retirement age if younger) or you are within six months of reaching that age. If there are objective grounds for turning you down then the employer can do so. One such ground is that you may not be able to work for a reasonably long enough period after training.

Finally, if there is a genuine occupational reason for turning you down such as needing a younger person to act in a role.

Running your own business

Retirement can be an opportunity to start your own business, perhaps turning a hobby into a business or trying something else completely new. This could be pursuing a dream, such as buying and selling property, self-publishing or whatever you have been developing or thinking about but didn't have the time to do when you were working.

Choosing the right business for you is not just a matter of thinking about the skills that you have. You should give serious thought to the work/life balance that you want to create. Some business take up a lot of time and can create a lot of stress, such as purchasing a shop. This in particular is likely to dominate your time and should, realistically, be avoided, unless you are absolutely certain about what you want to sell and where.

Business structure and tax

One of the first decisions is whether to set up a company, work in a partnership or go self-employed. By far the easiest route is to be self-employed. There are no formalities, such as setting up a company. You simply start trading, although you must register your business with HM Revenue and Customs within three months of the end of the month in which you start trading. You will have to fill in a tax return after the end of each tax year. Any profit that you make is added to your other income-such as pensions and any taxable investment income-to see if the total is high enough for you to have to pay tax.

Partnerships

From a tax point of view, partnerships are treated the same way as being self-employed. As with being self-employed, you have three months to register that you have started up and must complete an annual tax return. You should always try to have a formal agreement with any partners and get a solicitor to draw it up.

Trading as a company

This is the most top-heavy way of trading and there are a number of formalities to go through. These include forming a company, choosing a name and registering the company with Companies House who will require you to send in an annual return and also accounts each year. You will also need to contact your local tax office to tell them that you have started trading. By far and away the simplest form of business structure is that of self-employed and you should go this route if possible.

USEFUL ORGANISATIONS

MANAGING MONEY

Association of Investment
Trust Companies (AITC)
Durrant House
8-13 Chiswell Street
London EC1Y 4YY
Tel: 020 7285 5555
www.aitc.co.uk

Debt Management Office
Eastcheap Court
11 Philpot Lane
London EC3M 8UD
Tel: 0845 357 6500
www.dmo.gov.uk

Department forWork and Pensions (DWP)
If you ring The Pension Service on 0845 606 0265,
You will be connected to the pension centre covering you area,

Or you can look on the website (www.
Thepensionservice.gov.uk/contact)

Another useful DWP website is www.pensionguide.gov.uk

You can obtain DWP leaflets from Pension Service and
Jobcentre Plus office and some post offices, CABs or
Libraries.

You can write to:

Pension Guides
Freepost
Bristol BS38 7WA
Tel: 08457 31 32 33
If you have access to the Internet, you can download the leaflets
(and claim forms for many of the benefits)
from www.dwp.gov. uk or www.thepensionservice.gov.uk

Disability Alliance
Universal House
88-94 Wentworth Street
London E1 7SA
Tel: 020 7247 8776 www.disabilityalliance.org
Provides advice and publications on social security benefits
For disabled people.

Financial Ombudsman
Service (FOS)
South Quay Plaza
183 Marsh Wall
London E14 9SR
Consumer helpline: 0845 080 1800
www.financialombudsman.org,uk

Financial Services Authority (FSA)
25 The North Colonnade
Canary Wharf
London E14 5HS
Consumer helpline: 0845 606 1234
www.fsa.gov.uk/consummer

HM Revenue & Customs (HMRC)
The government department that deals

With almost all the taxes due in the UK.
Most HMRC leaflets can be obtained
From local tax offices or Tax Enquiry Centres
(look for in the phone book under 'Revenue'
or 'Government Department')
or Jobcentre Plus offices.
Almost all are also available on the website at:
www.hmrc.gov.uk or you can ring them the Orderline:
Tel: 0845 900 0404   or write to :
PO Box 37
St Austel
Cornwall PL25 5YN

HM Revenue & Customs National Insurance
Contributions Office (NICO)
Benton Park View
Newcastle upon Tyne NE98 1ZZ
Enquiry Line: 0845 300 1479

International Pension Centre
The Pension Service
Tyneview Park
Newcastle upon Tyne NE98 1BA
Tel: 0191 7777
(8.00am-8.00pm,weekdays)

Investment Management Association
65 Kingsway
London WC2B 6TD
Tel: 020 7831 0898
Information line 020 7269 4639
www.investmentfunds.org.uk
(OEIC.S).

MoneyFACTS
MoneyFacts House
66-70 Thorpe Road
Norwich NR1 1BJ
Tel: 0870 2250 100
www.moneyfactsgroup.co.uk

Office of the Public Guardian
Archway Tower
2 Junction Road
London N19 5SZ
Enquiry line: 0845 330 2900
Enduring Powers of Attorney: 0845 330 2963

The Pension Service
State Pension Forecasting Team
Future Pension Centre
Tyneview Park
Whitley Road Newcastle upon Tyne NE98 1BA
Tel: 0845 3000 168 www.thepensionservice.gove.uk

Pension Tracing Service
Tel: 0845 600 2537 www.thepensionservice.gov.uk

Pension Advisory Service
(TPAS)
11 Belgrave Road
London SW1V 1RB
Helpline: 0845 601 2923
www.pensionsadvisoryservice.org.uk

Principal Registry of the Family Division
(HM Courts Service)

First Avenue House
42-49 High Holborn
London WC1V 6NP
Tel: 020 7947 6000 www.courts-service.gov.uk
Wills can be lodged with the Probate Department ,
For a charge of £15. For information about
The leaflet `I want to deposit my will for safe
Keeping at the Principal Registry of the Family Division'.

Tax Help for Older People
Pineapple Business Park
Salway Ash
Bridport
Dorset DT6 5DB
Tel: 0845 601 3321 www.taxvol.org.uk

KEEPING ACTIVE

Age Concern England
1268 London Road
London SW16 4ER
020 8765 7200
www.ageconcern.org.uk

Association of British
Correspondence Colleges
PO Box 17926
London SW19 3WB
Tel: 020 8544 9559
www.homestudy.org.uk

Association of British Insurers (ABI)
51 Gresham Street
London EC2V 7HQ

Tel: 020 7600 0713
www.abi.org.uk

Association of British Travel
Agents (ABTA)
68-71 NEWMAN Street
London W1T 3AH
Tel: 020 7637 2444
www.abtanet.com

Association of Independent
Travel OPETATORS (AITO)
133A St Margaret's Road
Twickenham TW1 1RG
Tel: 020 8744 9280
www.aito.co.uk

British Franchise Association
(BFA)
Thames View
Newtown Road
Henley on Thames
Oxon RG9 1HG
Tel: 01491 578030
www.franchisedirect.com

British Trust for Conservation Volunteers
(BTCV)
Sedum House
Mallard Way
Doncaster DN4 8DB
Tel: 01302 388 883 www.btcv.org.uk
Camping and Caravanning

Club (CCC)
Greenfields House
Westwood Way
Coventry CV4 8JH
Tel: 0845 130 7631
www.campingandcaravanningclub.co.uk

Community Service
Volunteers (CSV)
237 Pentonville Road
London N1 9NJ
Tel: 020 7278 6601
www.cvs.org.uk

Cyclists' Touring Club
(CTC)
Parklands
Railton Road
Guildford
Surrey GU2 9JX
Tel: 0870 873 0060
www.ctc.org.uk

Department for Transport
Mobility and Inclusion Unit
Great Minster House
76 Marsham Street
London SW1P 4DR
Tel: 020 7944 8300
Blue Badge helpline: 020
7944 2914/0161 367 0009
www.dft.gov.uk

Disabled Persons Railcard
Office
PO Box 163
Newcastle upon Tyne
NE12 8WX
Tel:0845 605 0525
www.railcard.co.uk

Driver AND Vehicle Licensing
Department (DVLA)
DVLA Driver Customer
Services
Swansea SA6 7JL
Driver enquiries: 0870 240 0009
Textphone for Deaf and hard of Hearing 0300 123 0784
www.dvla.gov.uk
DVLA Vehicle Customer
Services
Vehicle enquiries: 0870 240
0010
www.dvla.gov.uk

European Health Insurance
Card (EHIC)
EHIC Enquiries
PO Box 1114
Newcastle upon Tyne NE99
2TL
Tel: 0845 605 0707
www.ehic.org.uk

Forum of Mobility Centre
C/o Providence Chapel

Warehorne
Ashford
Kent TN26 2JX
Tel: 0800 559 3636
(9.00am-5.00pm, weekdays)
www.mobility-centre.org.uk
A network of independent
Mobility centres that offer
Information, advice and
Assessment to people who
want to begin, or return to,
driving after illness, injury or accident.

Learndirect
Tel:0800 150 450
www.learndirect.co.uk
For free advice about all
Areas of learning and
Training.
Tel: 0800 101 901
www.learndirect-advice.co.uk

Lion World Travel Ltd/
Friendship Associations
Friendship House
49-51 Gresham Road
Staines
Middlesex TW18 2BF
Tel: 01784 465511
(8.00am-6.00pm,weekdays)
www.friendship-association.co.uk

Mobility Information Services
(MIS)
20 Burton Close
Dawley
Telford TF4 2BX
Tel: 01743 340269
www.mis.org.uk

Mobility
Motability Car Scheme
City Gate House
22 Southwark Bridge Road
London SE1 9HB
Tel: 0845 607 6260
(8.30am- 5.30pm,weekdays)
www.motability.co.uk

Motability Wheelchair and
Scooter Scheme
Route2mobility
Montgomery House
Newbury Road
Enham Alamein
Andover
Hampshire SP11 6JS

National Association of
Councils for Voluntary
And Community Service
(NACVS)
177 Arundel Street
Sheffield S1 2NU
Tel: 0114 278 6636 www.nacvs.org.uk

National Federation of
Women's Institutes (NFWI)
104 New Kings Road
London SW6 4LY
Tel: 020 7371 9300
www.nfwi.org.uk

National Institute of Adult
Continuing Education
(NIACE)
Renaissance House
20 Princess Road West
Leicester LE1 6TP
Tel: 0116 204 4200/4201
www.niace.org.uk

National Trust
PO Box 39
Warrington WA5 7WD
Tel: 0844 800 1895
www.nationaltrust.org.uk

Open College of the Arts
Registration Department
OCA
Freepost SF10678
Tel: 0800 731 2116
www.oca-uk.com
Open University (OU)
PO Box 197
Milton Keynes MK7 6BJ
Tel: 0845 300 6090 www.open.ac.uk

Age Concern England
1268 London Road
London SW16 4ER
Helpline: 0800 783 1904
Tel: 020 8765 7200
www.primeinitiative.org.uk

RADAR (Royal Association
For Disability and Rehabilitation)
12 City Forum
250 City Road
London EC1V 8AF
Tel: 020 7250 3222
www.radar.org.uk

Ramblers' Association
2nd Floor
Camelford House
87-90 Albert Embankment
London SE1 7TW
Tel: 020 7339 8500 www.ramblers.org.uk

REACH
89 Albert Embankment
London SE1 7TP
Tel: 020 7582 6543 www.reach-online.org.uk

Retired and Senior Volunteer
Programme (RSVP)
237 Pentonville Road
London N1 9NJ
Tel: 020 7643 1385
www.csv-rsvp.org.uk

The Age Employment
Network (TAEN)
207-221 Pentonville Road
London N1 9UZ
Tel: 020 7843 1590
www.taen.org.uk

Third Age Trust (U3A)
The Old Municipal Buildings
19 East Street
Bromley
Kent BR1 1QE
Tel: 020 8466 6139
(9.30am-1.30pm, weekdays)
www.u3a.org.uk

Tourism for All c/oVitalise
Shap Road Industrial Easte
Shap Road
Kendal
Cumbria LA9 6NZ
Tel: 0845 124 9971
www.tourismforall.org.ul

Townswoman
1st Floor
329 Tyburn Road
Birmingham B24 8HJ
Tel: 0121 326 0400
www.townswoman.org.uk

Voluntary Service Overseas
(VSO)
317 Putney Bridge Road
London SW15 2PN
Tel: 020 8780 7200
www.vso.org.uk

Volunteering England
Regent's Wharf
8 All Saints Street
London N1 9RL
Tel: 0845 305 6979
www.volunteeringengland.org.uk

Walking Women
22 Duke Street
Leamington Spa
Warwick CV32 4TR
Tel: 01926 313321
www.walkingwomen.com

Worker's Educational
Association (WEA)
3RD Floor
70 Clifton Street
London EC2A 4HB
Tel: 020 7426 3450
www.wea.org.uk

Working for a Charity
NCVO
Regent's Wharf
8 All Saints Street

London N1 9RL
Tel:020 7520 2512
www.workingforcharity.org.uk

RUNNING YOUR HOME

Abbeyfield Society
Abbeyfield House
53 Victoria Street
St Albans
Hertfordshire AL1 3UW
Tel: 01727 857536
www.abbeyfield.com

AIMS (Advice Information and
Mediation Service for
Retirement housing)
Astral House
1268 London Road
London SW16 4ER
Advice line: 0845 600 2001
www.ageconcern.org.uk/aims

Almshouse Association
Billingbear Lodge
Maidenhead Road
Wokingham
Berkshire RG40 5RU
Tel: 01344 452922 www.almshouses.org

Department for Environment,
Food and Rural Affairs
(DEFRA)

Pet Travel Scheme(PETS)
Eastbury House
30 –34 Albert Embankment
London SE1 7TL
Helpline: 08459 33 55 77
www.defra.gov.uk/animalh/quarantine

Disabled Living Foundation
(DLF)
380-384 Harrow Road
London W9 2HU
Helpline: 0845 130 9177
Demonstration centre:
0845 130 9177
Tel: 020 7289 6111
www.dlf.org.uk

Eaga Partnership Charitable
Trust (eaga plc)
Eage House
Archbold Terrace
Jesmond
Newcastle upon Tyne NE2 1DB
Tel: 0191 247 3800
www.eaga.co.uk

Elderly Accommodation
Counsel (EAC)
3rd Floor
89 Albert Embankment
London SE1 7TP
Adviceline: 020 7820 1343
www.housingcare.org

Energywatch
Percy House
Percy Street
Newcastle upon Tyne NE1
4PW
Helpline: 0845 906 0708
www.energywatch.org.uk

Federation of Master Builders (FMB)
Gordon Fisher House
14-15 Great James Street
London WC1N 3DP
Tel: 020 7242 7583
www.fmb.org.uk

Foundations (The national co-ordinating
body for home improvement agencies)
Bleaklow House
Howard Town Mill
Glossop SK13 8HT
Tel: 01457 891909
www.foundations.uk.com

Home Improvement Trust
7 Mansfield Road
Nottingham NG1 3FB
Tel: 0800 783 7569
www.hitrust.org

National House Building
Council (NHBC)
NHBC House
Davy Avenue

Knowlhill
Milton Keynes MK5 8FP
Tel: 0844 633 100
www.nhbc.co.uk

Trust Mark
Englemere
Kings Ride
Ascot SL5 7TB
Tel:0870 163 7373
www.trustmark.org.uk

STAYING HEALTHY

Ageing Well UK
Age Concern England
1268 London Road
London SW16 4ER
Information line:0800 00 99 66
www. Ageconcern.org.uk/

Arthritis Care
18 Stephenson Way
London NW1 2HD
Helpline: 0808 800 4050
Tel: 020 7380 6500
www.athritiscare.org.uk

Breast Cancer Care
210 New Kings Road
London SW6 4NZ
Helpline:0808 800 6000
www.breastcancercare.org.ul

British Dental Health Foundation
Smile House
2 East Union Street
Rugby
Warwickshire CV22 6AJ
Helpline: 0845 063 1188
Tel: 01788 539793
www.dentalhealth.org.uk

British Heart Foundation
14 Fitzhardinge Street
London W1H 6DH
Information line: 0845 070 8070
Tel: 020 7935 0185
www.bhf.org.uk

Cancerbackup
3 Bath Place
Rivingtin Street
London EC2A 3JR
Helpline: 0808 800 1234
(9am-8pm, weekdays)
Textphone: 18001 0808 800 1234
www.cancerbackup.org.uk

Diabetes UK
Macleod House
10 Parkway
London NW1 7AA
Careline: 0845 120 2960
Tel: 020 7424 1000
www.diabetes.org.uk

Hearing Concern
95 Gray's Inn Road
London WC1X 8TX
HelpDesk: 0845 0744 600
(voice & text)
Tel: 020 7440 9871
Textphone:020 7440 9873 {?1}
www.hearingconcern.org.uk

Incontact
SATRA Innovation Park
Rockingham Road
Kettering NN16 9JH
Helpline:01536 526 403
www.incontact.org

Institute of Trichologists
Ground Floor Office
24 Langroyd Road
London SW17 7PL
Tel: 0870 607 0602
www.trichologists.org.uk
Keep Fit Association
1 Grove House
Foundry Lane
Horsham
West Sussex RH13 5PL
Tel: 01493 266000
Also 0800 808 5252
www.keepfit.org.uk

National Osteoporosis
Society (NOS)

Manor Farm
Skinners Hill Camerton Bath BA2 OPJ
Tel: 01761 471771
Helpline: 0845 450 0230
www.nos.org.uk

NHS DIRECT
Tel:0845 46 47
Nhsdirect.nhs.uk
24- hour telephone and on line advice

NHS Drinkline
Freephone: 0800 917 8282
(9.00am- 11.00pm, weekdays)

Patients Association
PO Box 935
Harrow
Middlesex HA1 3YJ
Helpline: 0845 608 4455
Tel: 020 8423 9111
www.patientsassociation.com

Royal National Institute of BLIND People (RNIB)
105 Judd Street
London WC1H 9NE
Helpline: 0845 766 9999
Tel: 020 7388 1266
www.rnib.org.uk

Royal National Institute for
Deaf People (RNID)
19-23 Featherstone Street

London EC1Y 8SL
Information Line: 0808 808 0123
Textphone Helpline:0808 808 9000
www.rnid.org.uk

DEVELOPING RELATIONSHIPS

British Association for
Counselling and
Psychotherapy (BACP)
BACP House
15 St John's Business Park
Lutterworth
Leicestershire LE17 4HB
Tel: 01455 883300
www.bacp.co.uk

British Association for
Sexual and Relationship
Therapy
PO Box 13686
London SW10 9ZH
Tel: 020 8543 2707
www.basrt.org.uk

British Humanist Association
1 Gower Street
London WC1E 6HD
Tel: 020 7079 3580
www.humanism.org.uk

Carers UK
20 Great Dover Street
London SE1 4LX
Carersline: 0808 808 7777
Tel: 020 7378 4920
www.carersuk.org

Commission for Social Care Inspection (CSCI)
33 Greycoat Street
London SW1P 2QE
Helpline: 0845 015 0120
Tel: 020 7979 2000
www.csci.org.uk

Counsel and Care
Twyman House
16 Bonny Street
London NW1 9PG
Advice Line: 0845 300 7585
Tel: 020 7241 8555
www.counselandcare.org.uk

Crossroads Caring for carers
10 Regent Place
Rugby CV21 2PN
Helpline: 0845 450 0350 www.crossroads.org.uk

Cruse-Bereavement Care
PO Box 800 Richmond
Surrey TW9 1RG
Helpline: 0870 167 1677
Tel: 020 8939 9530
www.crusebereavementcare.org.uk

Family Rights Group
2nd Floor
The Print House
18 Ashwin Street
London E8 3DL
Advice Line: 0800 7311 696
Tel: 020 7923 2628
www.frg.org.uk

Grandparents' Association
Moot House
The Stow
Harlow
Essex CM20 3AG
Helpline: 0845 4349 585
Tel: 0279 428040 www.grandparentsassociation.org.uk

Grandparents Plus
18 Victoria Park Square
London E2 9PF
Tel: 020 8981 8001 www.grandparentsplus.org.uk

Relate
Premier House
Caroline Court
Lakeside Doncaster DN4 5RA
Tel: 0300 100 1234 www.relate.org.uk

United Kingdom Home
Care Association (UKHCA)
2nd Floor Group House
52 Sutton Court Road
Sutton Surrey SM1 4SL

Tel: 020 8288 5291
www.ukhca.co.uk

WRVS (Women's Royal
Voluntary Service)
Garden House
Milton Hill
Abingdon OX13 6AD
Tel: 01235 442900 www.wrvs.org.uk

Index